BALABOOSTA

BALABOOSTA

BOLD MEDITERRANEAN RECIPES
to Feed the People You Love

❖

EINAT ADMONY

With Joel Chasnoff *and* Dhale Pomes

Photography *by* Quentin Bacon

ARTISAN
NEW YORK

Published by Artisan

A division of Workman Publishing Company, Inc.

225 Varick Street

New York, NY 10014-4381

artisanbooks.com

Published simultaneously in Canada by Thomas Allen and Son, Limited.

Library of Congress Cataloging-in-Publication Data

Admony, Einat.

Balaboosta / Einat Admony with Joel Chasnoff and Dhale Pomes ; photography by Quentin Bacon.

pages   cm

Includes an index.

ISBN 978-1-57965-500-6

1. Cooking, Mediterranean. 2. Cooking, Israeli. I. Chasnoff, Joel.

II. Pomes, Dhale. III. Title.

TX725.M35A36   2013

641.59'1822—dc23

2013004900

Designed by Paul Kepple and Ralph Geroni at Headcase Design

Printed in China

First printing, August 2013

1 3 5 7 9 10 8 6 4 2

To Stefan

CONTENTS

THE FIRST CUT IS THE DEEPEST: Foods That Comfort — 89

JUST THE TWO OF US: Romantic Dishes — 109

THE BACKYARD BARBECUE: Recipes Best Enjoyed Outdoors — 130

INTRODUCTION

Long before I won *Chopped* or appeared on *Throwdown with Bobby Flay,* before there was cooking school, a husband, a better husband, and a couple of kids, before I ever imagined running three restaurants of my own in New York City, there were Friday afternoons with my mother.

O, THOSE UNFORGETTABLE FRIDAYS. They were hell—at least at first. Me: eight years old, in shorts and a tank top, sweating on my hands and knees as I scrubbed the kitchen floor with a dishrag. My mom: flying from stove to counter to fridge as she sliced vegetables, basted a chicken, and kneaded dough for the Sabbath challah. Then, just as suddenly, she'd move on to the living room, where she'd vacuum the rug with one hand and iron my father's shirt with the other. Around three o'clock on these Fridays, my friends would show up on the sidewalk outside our tiny Bnei Brak apartment. "Admohhhhneeee!" they'd scream. I'd look at my mother. "Please," my eyes would beg. Without missing a beat, she'd click her tongue—Israeli for "Don't even think about it!"—and send me to the bathroom to fetch a mop.

After four years of slave labor, my mother finally promoted me from indentured servant to sous-chef. Standing side by side at the stove, we plucked feathers out of raw chickens and scoured lettuce for microscopic worms. We roasted potatoes, fried fish, sautéed lamb, baked cakes, and ground our own hummus—all without the aid of a cookbook, measuring spoon, or timer. Instead, we relied on my mother's Persian instincts and the knowledge she'd inherited from generations of Jewish housewives before her. It was there, in my childhood kitchen, that I learned the trust-your-gut, *balaboosta* style of cooking that I rely on to this day.

ba·la·boo´·sta (n.)—a perfect housewife (Yiddish).

When I was a kid, I heard the word *balaboosta* all the time. I'm told it's derived from the Yiddish expression *baal habayit*—"owner of the house." Kind of ironic, since it was the men, not the women, who held the deeds to their shtetl homes. But also revealing, because we all know that, even today, it's the mothers who truly run the home.

Still, *balaboosta* didn't refer just to any ol' run-of-the-mill, hyperefficient housewife. It was a term of respect and endearment, reserved for the most energetic of women who tirelessly cooked and cleaned while taking charge of the spiritual and emotional well-being of their husbands and kids. A *balaboosta* made sure her table was crowded not just with food but also with laughter.

I come from a long line of *balaboostas.* There's my mom, Ziona, of course. There's her sister, Chana—a divorced mother of five who still spends eighteen hours a day making meatballs, rice, couscous, lamb stew, and chicken schnitzel for her kids, grandkids, neighbors, mailman, the old woman in the wheelchair across the hall, and whoever else might drop by for a bite.

Like my mom, my aunt Chana, and the generations of *balaboostas* before them, I cook from the gut: no measuring cups, no scales. But unlike them, I see being a *balaboosta* not just as a way to run a home but as a way of life. To be a twenty-first-century *balaboosta* means navigating the pitfalls of life with a courageous heart, a head filled with determination, and a spirit of risk and adventure. The modern *balaboosta* can be anyone—young or old, male or female, religious or not—who lives life with gusto, shuns fear, and relies on instinct over precision.

I'm thinking of my pal Amir—a man who left Israel in his twenties to pursue a career as a financial adviser in the States, working eighty hours a week and still managing to cook amazing dinners for friends a few times a month. I always look forward to his dinner parties—not just because of our friendship, but because he's the best nonprofessional chef I know and his passion for food is unreal. He's a true *balaboosta*.

And my dear friend Amy—a mother of two who launched a business whose mission is to empower women entrepreneurs. She was struck with breast cancer at age thirty-seven. But one mastectomy and four months of chemotherapy later, Amy has survived, her business is thriving, and she's even found the time to write a book. A modern *balaboosta* if ever there was one.

As for me—

I have two children under age seven, I run three restaurants in Manhattan (Balaboosta, Taïm and Taïm Mobile, and Bar Bolonat), I have a pretty good marriage, and I love to invite close friends for dinner several times a week. Like my aunt Chana, I pride myself on being the one who feeds everybody without asking anything in return except to see them happy. To me, that's what being a *balaboosta* is all about: emotion expressed through food. Not exactly my great-grandmother's definition of a perfect housewife, but a *balaboosta* all the same.

It's for these twenty-first-century *balaboostas* that I have written *Balaboosta*.

THE GROWN-UP TABLE

CASUAL
DINNER
PARTY
DISHES

I'm the only chef I know who cooks at home.

Okay, maybe not the only one.

But among my circle of chef friends, none go home after a long day at the restaurant and cook as elaborately—or as often—as I do.

AND WITH GOOD REASON. Who needs the hassle? Who wants to spend fourteen hours in a piping-hot kitchen, chopping, dicing, and slaving over a stove, only to go home and do it all over again?

But for me, cooking is more than a profession, or even a passion. It's my oxygen. My obsession. It is my window to creation, the linchpin of every relationship I have. And it's the best, and possibly only, way I know to truly give and receive love.

When my husband, Stefan, and I were first married, he was a waiter at Balthazar, a beloved French bistro in New York's SoHo. Most nights he wouldn't get home until two or three in the morning, and he would always be starving. (It's one of the ironies of the restaurant business—you leave work famished.) So I'd roll out of bed at whatever ungodly hour it was and make him a sandwich.

Now, that might not sound like a big deal. But you've never seen my sandwiches: thin slices of fresh turkey breast layered with caramelized onion, roasted red pepper, lettuce, and portobello mushrooms on toasted ciabatta bread slathered with homemade harissa aioli. I suppose I could have just ordered in Chinese. But that would never do. I couldn't bear the thought that my husband was hungry and that someone else—not I—would get to feed him. It's the same reason I have friends over at least three times a week. My colleagues call me crazy: "Isn't the stress of running a restaurant enough?" "Who in their right mind . . . ?"

But I'm not your typical chef. And my loved ones and I long ago gave up on the possibility that I was or ever would be in my right mind.

And so, a few times a week, I invite anywhere from two to thirty people to my Brooklyn apartment, where we enjoy a spread of appetizers, salads, entrées, wine, and desserts similar to what a customer would find on the Balaboosta menu. These gatherings give me a chance to try out new recipes on my unsuspecting lab-rat friends. But what I really love about having people over is the chatter, the laughter, the symphony of voices rising and falling in pitch over the clinking of glasses and the scrape of forks on plates—and knowing that my food is what brought us together.

Freud might say that this connection between love and food is a result of my first fistfight. I've been in exactly one fistfight in my life, when I was nine years old. Two younger girls from my elementary school accosted me outside my

apartment and beat me with their fists. (I still can't figure out how or why this happened.) What I remember most is not the searing pain I felt in my skull as knuckles cracked into my nose or the trickle of blood down my chin and shirt. No, what I remember most is the soup. After my mother soaked me in a warm bath and treated my cuts, she cooked me a bowl of *ahsh,* an Iranian soup made with pomegranates and rice. She then sat next to me at the kitchen table and stroked my hair as I ate, without saying a word.

She didn't have to. The *ahsh* said it all.

Call it medicine. Or nourishment. Or maybe just call it love. It is for the sake of this social bond, this wonderfully fulfilling opportunity to connect people, that I became a chef in the first place. And it's why I never cook for myself, only for others. What good is love if you partake of it alone?

The entrées and appetizers that follow can be mixed and matched to make a multicourse meal. They're ideal for sharing with your grown-up friends. While kids can certainly enjoy them too, these recipes are a tad on the spicy side. And anyway, they're best enjoyed over adult conversation.

ROSÉ SANGRIA

Makes about 5 cups

BEING MARRIED TO A FRENCH-man poses many challenges. But there are benefits too—like the way Stefan has helped foster my love for wine. For example, rosé to me had always tasted like something between a red and a white but never as good as either. Then Stef created this delicious rosé sangria for the Balaboosta menu. The peach puree adds an opaque pinkish color and great texture; without it, the wine would be too diluted. Best of all, the puree makes the sangria look like juice, which means no one has to know that you're getting tipsy at one in the afternoon.

1 cup frozen peaches, thawed
One 750-ml bottle rosé wine, chilled
⅓ cup Mint Syrup (page 278)
Ice
Fresh mint leaves
Lime wedges
Vodka (optional)

- Puree ¾ cup of the peaches and transfer to a large pitcher. Add the wine, the remaining peaches, and the mint syrup. Stir to combine.

- Serve over ice with fresh mint leaves and lime wedges. Whether you decide to add a splash or two of vodka is not my place to say.

CORN SALAD

Serves 4

I SEE VERSIONS OF THIS DISH everywhere in Israel, from my family's table to the buffet line at bar mitzvahs to the local deli. For those of you who don't like dill, try cilantro—it works just as well, and it'll give the salad a more Mexican character. Dill, meanwhile, has a strong aniselike flavor and is distinctly Mediterranean.

Sometimes I like to serve this as a warm salad, so I just pop it in the microwave for a minute or two right before serving.

⅓ cup distilled white vinegar

2 tablespoons extra virgin olive oil

1 tablespoon sugar

½ teaspoon kosher salt

¼ teaspoon freshly ground black pepper

3 cups corn kernels (6 medium ears, but frozen or canned corn works just as well)

2 red bell peppers, cored, seeded, and cut into small dice

2 jalapeño chiles, cored, seeded, and cut into small dice

¼ cup chopped fresh dill or 1½ tablespoons dried dill

- Whisk together the vinegar, olive oil, sugar, salt, and pepper. Add the corn, bell peppers, jalapeños, and dill and toss everything together.

SWEET NANA TEA

Makes about 5 cups

OH, NANA, HOW I LOVE THEE! Let me count the ways: in food, in alcohol, and even as a medicine. But at the end of the day, I'm convinced nana (fresh mint) was created for tea. For me, there's just no better way to finish a big dinner than with a mug of piping-hot mint tea. I use a combination of tea leaves—black and green—for a richer taste.

2 teaspoons green tea leaves

2 teaspoons black tea leaves

5 cups boiling water

¼ cup sugar

1 cup fresh mint

- Place the tea leaves in a teapot with 1 cup of the boiling water. Gently swirl around the water to warm the pot and rinse the leaves. Drain the water and reserve the leaves in the pot.

- Pour the remaining boiling water into the teapot and add the sugar. Stir until the sugar is completely dissolved. Add the mint leaves and steep for 5 minutes.

CASABLANCA CATCH

Serves 4

A SURE WAY TO MY HEART IS a North African fish recipe. There are dozens of ways to prepare it; in this version I combine my favorites into one. Sure, the sauce is oily, but Moroccans use oil in almost everything, so to remove it would be inauthentic. The preserved lemon melted around the chickpeas gives it a distinct kick, and the cilantro, my favorite herb, opens up the earthiness that comes from the combination of the oil and chickpeas, lightening the whole recipe. I love to serve this with challah on the side for sopping up the sauce.

$\frac{1}{2}$ cup dried chickpeas, soaked in water overnight, or 1 heaping cup drained canned chickpeas

$\frac{1}{2}$ cup canola oil

15 garlic cloves, thinly sliced

3 fresh chiles, cored, seeded and halved lengthwise (I use jalapeño, but you can use 2 long, skinny red ones)

2 red bell peppers, cored, seeded, and sliced into 2-inch strips

$\frac{1}{4}$ cup sweet Hungarian paprika

2 tablespoons World's Best Harissa (page 272)

4 skinless white fish fillets (bass, grouper, snapper, or tilapia), cut into twelve 4-inch pieces

4 to 6 Perfect Preserved Lemons (page 276)

$\frac{1}{2}$ cup fresh cilantro without tough stems

- Simmer the dried chickpeas in water to cover until not quite tender, about 1 hour (if using canned chickpeas, skip this step but rinse them thoroughly). Drain the chickpeas, reserving the cooking liquid. You can cover and refrigerate the chickpeas and the liquid separately overnight.

- Warm the oil in a large skillet or saucepan over medium heat. Add the garlic, chiles, bell peppers, and paprika. Stir until the peppers are coated really well and cook until soft and fragrant but not browned, about 15 minutes. Stir in the harissa and cook for a minute or so, just long enough to let the flavors meld.

- Meanwhile, pat the fish dry. Place it on a plate, squeeze the juice of one of the preserved lemons over the top, and let the fish soak for 5 minutes. Rinse the fish and pat it dry. Cut the remaining lemons into wedges.

- Scatter a handful of cilantro over the peppers and then arrange the fish on top. Pour just enough of the chickpea cooking liquid into the pan to reach halfway up the pieces of fish. Give the skillet a gentle shake.

- Add another handful of cilantro, then the preserved lemon wedges and the chickpeas. Cover and simmer very, very gently, so only an occasional bubble breaks the surface of the sauce. After 10 minutes, uncover the pan and let it continue to simmer gently until the liquid has reduced, 10 to 20 more minutes. You'll know the dish is ready when the chickpeas are perfectly tender, the fish is milky white throughout, and your house is filled with fragrance.

- Remove the skillet from the heat and toss one more handful of cilantro over the fish.

CHALLAH

Makes 4 loaves

WHAT'S WONDERFUL ABOUT challah is that it can be used in so many ways: to sanctify the Sabbath, of course, but just as important, to make French toast, grilled cheese, and croutons and as breading in meatballs. Maybe not the way God intended it, but I'm sure She understands. Israel is the land of milk and honey, and this challah has both. For those of you who want to stay away from milk, it's fine to substitute water.

2$\frac{1}{2}$ cups whole milk or water

8$\frac{2}{3}$ cups all-purpose flour, plus flour for the work surface

1$\frac{1}{2}$ tablespoons active dry yeast

$\frac{1}{2}$ cup honey or sugar

$\frac{1}{4}$ cup canola oil, plus more oil for the bowl

4 large eggs

1$\frac{1}{2}$ tablespoons kosher salt

White sesame or nigella seeds for sprinkling

- Heat the milk in a small saucepan over low heat just until it's warm to the touch. Remove from the heat.

- Dump the flour into a large bowl and make a well in the center. Add the yeast to the well along with a few drops of honey and $\frac{1}{2}$ cup or so of the warm milk. Let stand until foamy, about 10 minutes.

- In a separate bowl, combine the remaining milk and honey, the oil, and 3 of the eggs. Stir together. Add the salt and stir again. Gradually stir the liquid mixture into the flour, about $\frac{1}{2}$ cup at a time. When the dough becomes sticky and difficult to stir, dump onto a floured surface and knead it by hand, adding a little more flour if necessary to keep it from sticking, until smooth and elastic.

- Knead the dough into a ball. Slick another large bowl with oil, add the dough, and turn to slick the surface with oil. Cover with a damp cloth and let stand in a warm place until double in size, 1 to 1$\frac{1}{2}$ hours.

- Line 2 baking sheets with parchment paper. Gently punch the dough down and turn it onto a floured surface. Divide the dough into four equal portions, working with one portion at a time and keeping the rest covered with a damp cloth. Divide one portion of dough into three equal pieces and roll each piece into a rope about 1 foot long and slightly tapered at the ends. Line the ropes side by side on one side of the baking sheet and braid them, pinching the ends to seal and tucking them underneath. Repeat this process with the remaining dough until you have four nicely braided loaves. Cover with a damp cloth and let stand until nearly double in size, another 25 minutes or so.

- Preheat the oven to 350° F.

- Lightly beat the remaining egg and brush it over the tops of the challah loaves. Sprinkle with the nigella or sesame seeds. Bake the loaves until golden brown, 20 to 30 minutes.

SPICY CHICKEN TAGINE

Serves 4 to 6

IN MY NEXT LIFE, I WANT TO
be Moroccan. I just love the cooking
techniques, the spices, the tastes. My
elderly neighbor while I was growing
up, Tova, was Moroccan, and I'd often
stop by her apartment to watch her
cook (and to learn). The ingredients
used here are certainly ones that could
be found in many of Tova's dishes, but
I've combined them in a new way. The
mint in particular adds freshness to
what is otherwise a very rich dish.

1 orange

3 pounds chicken pieces with skin and bone, preferably
thighs and drumsticks

2 teaspoons kosher salt

½ teaspoon freshly ground black pepper

2 cups chicken stock

2 to 3 heaping tablespoons World's Best Harissa (page
272)

2 tablespoons sweet Hungarian paprika

1 tablespoon ground cumin

1 teaspoon ground turmeric (optional)

1 Perfect Preserved Lemon (page 276) or 1 fresh lemon,
cut into small wedges

10 garlic cloves, unpeeled

2 fennel bulbs, cut into ½-inch-thick wedges

2 leeks, white and light green parts only, or 1 yellow onion,
cut into 2-inch pieces

¾ cup black olives, pitted

1 cup fresh mint leaves, coarsely chopped or torn into
pieces

- Preheat the oven to 350°F.

- Slice the ends off the orange with a sharp knife. Stand the
fruit on the cutting board and slice off the peel with just a
tiny bit of the underlying pith by following the curve of the
fruit. Reserve the peel for later and squeeze the juice from
the orange. If it doesn't quite make 1 cup, just mix in a little
bit of store-bought orange juice or even water in a pinch.

- Season the chicken pieces with salt and pepper and set aside.
Put the chicken stock, orange juice, harissa, paprika, cumin,
and turmeric into a large Dutch oven or other heavy pot. Stir
well. Throw in the preserved lemon, orange peel, garlic cloves,
fennel, leeks, olives, half of the mint, and the chicken pieces.
Toss together until everything is coated really well.

- Turn the chicken skin side up and then bake in the covered
Dutch oven for 1 hour. Crank up the oven temperature to
425°F, remove the lid, and allow the skin to get crisp and the
juices to reduce, about 30 minutes.

- Just before you take the pot to the table, scatter the remaining mint leaves over the chicken.

COUSCOUS COUNTLESS WAYS

Serves 4 to 6

I COULD EAT COUSCOUS EVERY day for the rest of my life if I knew I wouldn't gain a single pound. And if I had to take one food to a deserted island, this would be it. Authentic couscous is extremely labor intensive, because it's rolled by hand, with water and oil added slowly, then strained and steamed—and then the whole thing is done all over again. I like to make the real deal, but just as often I'll compromise and make an instant version, varying it in numerous ways.

Crispy shallots are available in many Asian groceries.

1 box instant couscous (I prefer the Roland brand)

VARIATIONS TO ADD TO THE COOKING LIQUID
Cinnamon stick and bay leaf
1 teaspoon each sweet Hungarian paprika, ground cumin, and ground turmeric
Garlic cloves, thinly sliced

VARIATIONS FOR THE TOPPING
Crispy shallots and raisins
Sautéed almonds and currants
Crispy garlic and chopped dried apricots

1 tablespoon unsalted butter

- Prepare the couscous according to the package instructions, but try adding one of the variations to the cooking liquid. You can also use chicken broth instead of water.

- Top off the couscous with store-bought crispy shallots or try my favorite—sautéed almonds and raisins, which I always serve alongside the Spicy Chicken Tagine (page 29).

- Add the butter to the couscous, stir to mix, and fluff it up with a fork.

CAULIFLOWER EVERYONE LOVES

Serves 4 to 6

THIS CAULIFLOWER IS CRISPY, salty, sweet, and tangy. I use ground white and pink peppercorns in the flour mix to give a peppery flavor that's milder than if the pepper were black. This recipe evolved at Balaboosta—and judging by the number of e-mails I get requesting it, I think it's a hit.

WHITE WINE VINAIGRETTE
¼ cup white wine vinegar
2 tablespoons honey
1 teaspoon Dijon mustard
3 tablespoons extra virgin olive oil
2 teaspoons kosher salt
Pinch of freshly ground black pepper

CRISPY CAULIFLOWER
5 cups canola oil
1 large head cauliflower, cut into bite-sized florets
1 cup all-purpose flour
3 teaspoons kosher salt
1 teaspoon freshly ground white pepper
1 teaspoon freshly ground pink pepper
Dried currants (optional)
Toasted pine nuts (optional)
Coarsely chopped fresh parsley (optional)

For the Vinaigrette

- Whisk together the vinegar, honey, and mustard. Slowly drizzle in the olive oil while whisking to create an emulsion. Season with the salt and pepper. Set aside until ready to use.

For the Cauliflower

- In a large, heavy pot, heat the canola oil over medium heat until the temperature reaches 350°F.

- Meanwhile, bring a large pot of water to a boil. To blanch the cauliflower, prepare an ice bath in a large bowl and keep it next to the stove. Working in small batches, plunge the cauliflower florets into the boiling water for 2 minutes and drop them into the ice bath. Repeat until all the florets are blanched.

- Combine the flour, salt, and white and pink pepper in a large resealable plastic bag. Throw in the florets, seal the bag, and shake, shake, shake until thoroughly coated.

- Working in small batches again, carefully drop the florets into the hot oil and fry until golden brown, 3 to 5 minutes. Using a slotted spoon, transfer the florets to paper towels to drain.

- Transfer to a serving dish and drizzle the vinaigrette over the crispy cauliflower.

- Toss together the cauliflower, vinaigrette, and a tiny handful of currants, pine nuts, and parsley right before serving.

MOROCCAN CARROTS

Serves 4 to 6

WHEN I OPENED TAÏM, I PUT as much effort into the recipe for carrot salad as into the one for falafel. Here I sauté the carrots with tomato paste, giving them a robust color and texture. The tomato paste also provides an unexpectedly sweet coating that's a counterpoint to the acidity of the vinegar.

2½ pounds carrots, cut into ¼-inch-thick coins
¼ cup extra virgin olive oil
¼ cup plus **2** tablespoons distilled white vinegar
2½ teaspoons kosher salt
1¼ teaspoons ground cumin
1 teaspoon sweet Hungarian paprika
½ teaspoon sugar
Pinch of cayenne
Pinch of freshly ground black pepper
3 garlic cloves, thinly sliced
1 tablespoon tomato paste

- Bring a large pot of water to a boil. To blanch the carrots, prepare an ice bath in a large bowl and keep it next to the stove. Once the water starts to boil, throw in the carrots and cook just until tender but still crisp, about 8 minutes. Scoop the carrots out of the boiling water and plunge into the ice bath. Once the carrots are completely cooled, drain the water and allow the carrots to dry for 5 to 10 minutes (being splattered with oil is never fun).

- While the carrots are cooking, whisk together 2 tablespoons of the olive oil, the vinegar, salt, cumin, paprika, sugar, cayenne, pepper, and garlic. Set aside.

- Heat the remaining 2 tablespoons olive oil in a skillet over medium heat and sauté the tomato paste in it for about 2 minutes. This will actually sweeten the tomato paste and make it less tangy. Add the carrots and sauté just until crispy, about 10 minutes. Remove the carrots from the heat, cool slightly, and add the vinegar mixture to the skillet. Toss everything together until coated really, really well.

MY HOMEMADE KIT KAT

Makes about 24 pieces

MY FIRST PROFESSIONAL CHEF job was as a line cook at Keren, which at the time was the top restaurant in Israel. Honestly, it was the best start a chef could ask for. Many years have passed since then. But this recipe for chocolate fingers will stay with me forever.

14 ounces 72% cacao chocolate, broken into tiny pieces
1 tablespoon unsalted butter
¾ cup Nutella
2 cups crushed cornflakes (about 3 cups whole)
1¾ cups heavy cream

- Fill a medium saucepan three-quarters full with water and bring to a simmer. Combine 1 ounce of the chocolate with the butter in a large bowl. Place the bowl over the saucepan and slowly melt the chocolate and butter together, stirring occasionally with a rubber spatula. Remove from the heat, reserving the pan of hot water, and stir in the Nutella. Cool completely, then mix in the crushed cornflakes. Spread this mixture evenly in a 9-by-13-inch baking pan and reserve in the refrigerator until the coating is ready.

- Bring the saucepan of hot water back to a simmer. Combine the remaining 13 ounces chocolate and the heavy cream in a large bowl and place it over the saucepan. Stir the mixture occasionally with a rubber spatula to combine the melting chocolate with the heavy cream. Remove from the heat and slowly pour the ganache over the crispy Nutella mixture. Place the baking pan in the refrigerator until the chocolate is completely set and firm. Cut into finger-sized rectangles and watch them disappear in minutes.

CHEESECAKE

WITH

MEYER LEMON GLAZE

Makes one 9-inch cake,
12 to 16 slices

MY MOTHER HAS MANY
strengths in the kitchen, but baking
was never among them. The one exception was her cheesecake. I remember
how hot it was coming out of the oven
and how I couldn't wait until the cake
chilled, so I could dig in at the hard
crust before my mom noticed. The recipe here calls for low-fat cheese—it's
a bit healthier, sure, but the real benefit is that it makes the cake lighter
and fluffier. If you're running short
on time, take a shortcut to the super-
market for a premade crust.

Meyer lemons are available only
for a short period of time in the winter; out of season, use the juice from
regular lemons or tangerines.

CRUST
1¼ cups all-purpose flour, plus flour for the work surface
⅓ cup sugar
Pinch of kosher salt
8 tablespoons (1 stick) cold unsalted butter, cut into small cubes
1 tablespoon sour cream or yogurt

FILLING
6 large eggs, separated
1½ cups sugar
Two 8-ounce packages low-fat cream cheese, at room temperature
14 ounces sour cream
¼ cup milk
¼ cup all-purpose flour
¼ cup cornstarch
¼ cup instant vanilla pudding mix (about ¾ packet)

MEYER LEMON GLAZE
5 egg yolks
¾ cup sugar
⅓ cup fresh Meyer lemon juice (about 4 lemons)
8 tablespoons (1 stick) cold unsalted butter, cut into small cubes

For the Crust

- Combine the flour, sugar, salt, and butter in a food processor. Pulse until the mixture looks like coarse sand. Add the
sour cream and pulse a few more times. Remove the dough
from the food processor and knead it a little with your hands.
Shape it into a disk about 3 inches in diameter, wrap it in
plastic wrap, and refrigerate for 30 minutes.

- Preheat the oven to 350°F.

- Remove the dough from the refrigerator and lightly flour the
surface of your work area. Flatten the dough using a rolling
pin (a wine bottle works just as well) until it just overlaps the
outer edges of a 9-inch springform pan. Use the bottom of the
pan to press down onto the dough like a cookie cutter. Reas-
semble the pan and gently press the dough into the bottom.

Continued

- Bake the crust until golden brown, about 10 minutes. Remove from the oven to cool slightly, then place it in the refrigerator to chill for at least 1 hour. This step can be done up to a day in advance.

For the Filling

- Preheat the oven to 325°F.

- Beat the egg yolks and 1 cup of the sugar together with an electric mixer until light yellow and fluffy. Next add the cream cheese, sour cream, and milk until well combined. Add the flour and cornstarch and mix until smooth and creamy. Transfer this mixture to a large bowl using a rubber spatula.

- In a clean mixing bowl, whip the egg whites with the electric mixer until soft peaks form. With the beater running, gradually add the remaining $1/2$ cup sugar and keep whipping until stiff peaks form, about 5 minutes. Reduce the mixer speed to low and slowly pour in the cheesecake filling from the other bowl. Next add the instant pudding mix and mix just until thoroughly combined.

- Remove the cheesecake pan from the refrigerator and pour the filling over the crust. Bake until the cheesecake is set, 45 to 50 minutes, until a toothpick inserted in the center of the cheesecake comes out clean. Remove from the oven and cool to room temperature.

For the Meyer Lemon Glaze

- Fill a medium saucepan three-quarters full with water and bring to a simmer. While the water is heating, combine the egg yolks and sugar in a large bowl and whip together with an electric mixer until light yellow and fluffy. Once the water comes to a simmer, place the bowl over the pan and stir in the lemon juice with a rubber spatula. Keep stirring until the mixture is thick enough to coat the back of a spoon.

- Remove from the heat and quickly whisk in the cubes of butter one piece at a time until completely dissolved. Pour over the baked cheesecake, cover the pan with plastic wrap (make sure the plastic is not touching the glaze), and place in the refrigerator until the glaze is set, about 6 hours. Carefully release the sides of the pan, transfer the cake to a plate, and slice.

KIDDING AROUND

RECIPES
TO
FEED
YOUR KIDS

When it came to feeding their middle child, my mom and dad were the luckiest Jewish parents on earth:

I ate everything.

CHICKEN HEARTS? I GOBBLED THEM WHOLE. Bull-testicle soup at Zacharia's restaurant? I slurped it down and licked the saucer clean. I didn't just devour food; I savored it, cracking shank bones with my tiny hands and sucking the juice off my nails. In a country notorious for its lack of manners, I was an animal.

The one exception was liver.

Once a month, my mother cooked a chicken liver for supper. First she salted it, to make it kosher. Then, just in case any hint of flavor remained, she scorched it under the broiler, while I watched in horror, as every last droplet of juice dripped into the pan.

Even worse than the taste of the liver was my mother's motivation for cooking it. My mom prepared most dinners with my older sister, Dorit, in mind. Dorit was skinny, and my parents did anything they could to add weight to her skeletal frame, even if it meant scooping food off my plate and hand-feeding it to her.

But every so often my mother broiled a chicken liver especially for me. She was convinced I was anemic—a diagnosis based not on blood tests but on her Persian intuition. Liver Night was the one meal when my parents stole food from Dorit and offered the spoils to me.

Thanks, but no thanks. I made up my mind, then and there, that if I ever had children of my own I would never, ever make them eat liver.

Fast-forward thirty years and six thousand miles west. It's March 2006, and my beautiful son, Liam, has just nursed for the first time. As he sleeps in my arms, I make a silent pledge that breast milk will be the one and only kid-friendly food he will ever eat. Once I wean my baby, he will eat like a grown man.

Mostly, it's worked. Liam's seven now, and he enjoys oysters and artichoke hearts and takes his steak medium-rare. His five-year-old sister, Mika, likes mussels. And I hate to brag, but both absolutely love liver (sorry, Mom)—not because my children love me more than I loved my own mother, but because I "schnitzel" the liver (fillet, bread, spice, and fry it) instead of broiling it dry (see Chicken Littles, page 53).

The recipes in this chapter are based on my belief that there's no such thing as kid foods and grown-up foods. Instead, there are only our memories of not liking, say, asparagus and our assumption that our own children won't either.

Not so. Just as a toddler can learn any language, a child's palate is open. So not only *can* you introduce your child to a variety of tastes, you are *obliged* to do so. Otherwise, you deprive him or her of the opportunity to savor the abundance of spices and flavors the world has to offer.

However, I can offer a few words about child-friendly food prep:

Taste matters to kids, but so do texture and color. If it's mushy and bland, my kids won't eat it. I stick with firm, brightly colored foods instead. Be advised that cooking healthfully for kids can necessitate some stealthiness on your part. In Sneaky Noodles (page 58), I grate the vegetables into the sauce—a way to get your kids (and mine) to eat a balanced meal and expand their palates without their knowing it.

Whenever possible, allow your children to cook with you. Kids are more likely to eat what they've helped prepare. And at the risk of hurting my business as a restaurant owner, I'll share a second benefit to cooking with your child: independence. Kids who cook grow into adults who don't need to rely on restaurants for a healthy meal. (Except Balaboosta, 214 Mulberry Street, NYC, 212-966-7366. Reservations accepted.)

Some ideas for cooking with kids:

1. Provide your child with a special apron or, better, a pint-sized chef's jacket with his name stitched on the pocket.

2. Lay out all ingredients beforehand.

3. Know ahead of time what your child can and cannot do. (Easy as it sounds, it's hard for a five-year-old to crack an egg.)

4. Kids love the tactile sensation of new foods in their hands. Allow them to knead raw beef and stretch dough between their fingers—but be sure they don't swallow uncooked dough.

Best of all, when you cook for your kids, you teach them about what's always attracted me to the kitchen in the first place: the pride that comes from providing someone you love with a meal you created, so long as it's not my mother's liver.

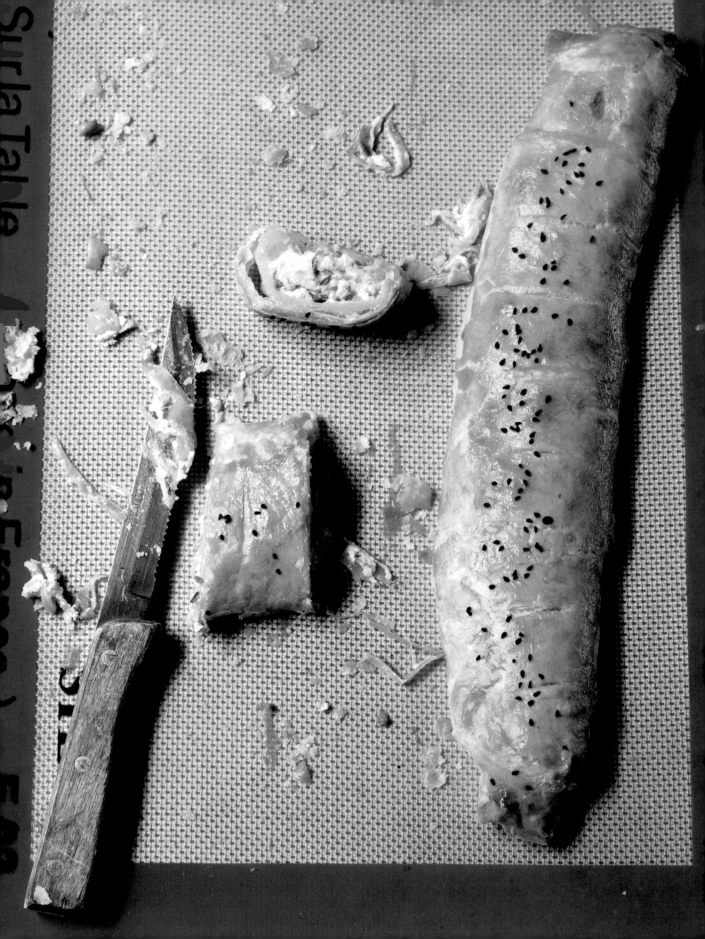

BOUREKAS

Makes 10 pieces

BOUREKAS ARE ONE OF THE most popular foods from my childhood—probably because you can't attend a wedding or bar mitzvah in Israel without encountering them. They're baked puff pastries that are traditionally filled with either potatoes, mushrooms, spinach, or cheese. They're usually served with mushroom gravy as an appetizer option, but these are a darn good second choice—no rite of passage required.

Nigella seeds can be found in gourmet markets, but if they're not available, you can substitute white or black sesame seeds.

CARAMELIZED ONIONS

4 tablespoons (½ stick) butter
2 medium yellow onions, thinly and evenly sliced
1 tablespoon kosher salt

BOUREKAS

One 8-ounce package mild fresh goat cheese, at room temperature
1½ cups whole-milk ricotta
4 dried apricots, cut into very small cubes
2 tablespoons finely chopped fresh thyme
⅛ teaspoon grated nutmeg
Pinch of freshly ground black pepper
1 tablespoon kosher salt
One 17.3-ounce package puff pastry, thawed (my go-to brand is Pepperidge Farm)
All-purpose flour for the work surface
1 large egg, beaten
Nigella seeds

For the Caramelized Onions

- Heat a large skillet over medium heat and melt the butter in it. Add half of the onions and sprinkle 1½ teaspoons of the salt over them. Add the remaining onions and the remaining 1½ teaspoons of salt. Resist the urge to stir the onions during the first 15 minutes of cooking, because leaving them alone will help with the caramelization. Allow the onions to stick to the pan just slightly, then give them a quick stir.

- Reduce the heat to low and stir occasionally to prevent the onions from burning. Cook until a deep, rich brown color has developed. Remove from the heat and cool completely. (The onions can be stored in an airtight container in the refrigerator for up to 1 day.)

For the Bourekas

- Line a baking sheet with parchment paper—if you have a Silpat, even better.

Continued

- Mix together the goat cheese, ricotta, dried apricots, caramelized onions (about 1 cup), thyme, nutmeg, pepper, and salt.

- Unroll one puff pastry sheet on a lightly floured surface. Take half of the goat cheese mixture and spread a thick horizontal line across the sheet on the end closest to you. Tightly roll the puff pastry into a large log. Repeat this step with the second sheet. Transfer both rolls to the lined baking sheet and refrigerate for 30 minutes.

- Preheat the oven to 375°F. Remove the rolls from the refrigerator and brush the tops with the egg; sprinkle with the nigella seeds. Divide each roll into five equal pieces by making a $\frac{1}{4}$-inch-deep incision using a very sharp knife. Bake in the oven until golden brown, about 35 minutes.

- Remove the *bourekas* from the oven and cut all the way through the slits of each roll. Serve immediately.

CHICKEN LITTLES

Serves 4 to 6

THIS IS MY VERSION OF chicken nuggets, or, as it's known in Israel, schnitzel. Schnitzel is second only to falafel in terms of popularity in Israel, although we make it with chicken, not the veal in the original Austrian version. My friends and I grew up with mothers who got jobs in order to help supplement their husbands' income—but these forward-thinking moms weren't ready to abandon their dreams of running a perfect household. Schnitzel was a convenient way for working mothers to serve a hot meal that was also nutritious. You'll notice I use cornflakes—they give the chicken some extra crunch—and I use panko because it holds better than traditional bread crumbs. If you want to get some iron into your kids, use chicken liver instead of chicken tenders.

2 pounds chicken tenders or chicken livers
Kosher salt
Freshly ground black pepper
Canola oil for frying
1 cup all-purpose flour
3 large eggs, beaten
1 cup crushed cornflakes (about 1½ cups whole)
1 cup panko or regular dried bread crumbs

- Rinse the chicken tenders and pat them dry. Season with salt and pepper and set aside.

- Fill a deep skillet with about 1 inch of oil. Heat until the temperature reaches 350°F.

- Meanwhile, create an assembly line consisting of three bowls: the first bowl with the flour, the second with the eggs, and the third with the cornflakes and panko combined. Working with one tender at a time, dip it first into the flour and dust off the excess. Next coat it in the egg, and then toss it in the cornflake mixture. Repeat with all the chicken tenders.

- Gently place the chicken tenders in the hot oil, working in batches if necessary. Fry for 3 minutes on each side, until they are golden and crispy.

AHOOVA'S PATTIES

Makes about 12 patties

AHOOVA IS A STATUESQUE Ethiopian-Israeli woman who took care of my children until my youngest, Mika, began nursery school. She's a special part of Liam and Mika's life—and mine. Ahoova claimed she couldn't cook, but then one evening I discovered her making meat patties from scratch. It turned out the recipe was mine, but I'd never added sweet potato until I saw Ahoova do it. It's a genius move, because it makes the patties moist, sweet, and colorful.

1 pound ground beef
$\frac{1}{2}$ medium yellow onion, finely chopped
1 medium carrot, finely grated
1 medium sweet potato, boiled and mashed (about 1 cup)
1 large egg, beaten
$\frac{1}{2}$ teaspoon ground cumin
$\frac{1}{2}$ teaspoon sweet Hungarian paprika
1 teaspoon kosher salt
$\frac{1}{2}$ teaspoon freshly ground black pepper
$\frac{1}{4}$ cup chopped fresh flat-leaf parsley
1 cup crumbs made from Challah (page 24)
Canola oil

- Combine the ground beef, onion, carrot, sweet potato, egg, cumin, paprika, salt, pepper, and parsley. Mix together, using your hands. Add the bread crumbs.

- Shape the beef mixture into 2-inch patties. Heat a large skillet with oil and fry for 5 minutes on each side.

PTITIM

(ISRAELI COUSCOUS)

Serves 4 to 6

ISRAELI COUSCOUS IS NOT actually couscous—it's toasted pasta shaped like little balls. The recipe was developed in the 1950s as a replacement for rice. It very quickly became a beloved and tasty, easy-to-prepare dish adored by children and moms alike throughout the country. In the United States, however, Israeli couscous is served in fine-dining establishments. Isn't it amazing how the same food can have a completely different use from one culture to the next? If your kids are anything like mine, they'll love the taste of this popular dish. You can elevate the basic recipe by adding cinnamon, paprika, turmeric, or countless other spices.

2 tablespoons canola oil
1 medium yellow onion, finely chopped
2 cups Israeli couscous
2 teaspoons kosher salt
3 cups vegetable broth

- Heat the oil in a medium saucepan over medium heat. Add the onion and sauté just until translucent, about 7 minutes. Add the couscous and salt and sauté for another 2 minutes. Add the vegetable broth and bring to a boil. Lower the heat and cook just until the liquid has evaporated, about 10 minutes. Remove from the heat and serve immediately to your hungry little bears.

CATCH-UP CHICKEN

Serves 4

I RAISED MY KIDS ON THE principle that ketchup isn't a solution; it's an indication: if my children don't like something, they shouldn't add ketchup—they simply shouldn't eat it in the first place. But this recipe is one that purposely highlights the ketchup, giving the chicken a sweet and tangy flavor reminiscent of what you'd get at a backyard cookout. This way you can give your kids a barbecue experience without the smoke and the drunk uncle.

1 cup ketchup

½ cup apple juice

1 tablespoon kosher salt

2 teaspoons ground cumin

1 teaspoon sweet Hungarian paprika

3 pounds bone-in chicken pieces, skin on

1 medium yellow onion, cut into large chunks

2 tomatoes, cut into wedges

- Preheat the oven to 350°F.

- Mix together the ketchup, apple juice, salt, cumin, and paprika in a large Dutch oven or other heavy pot.

- Rinse the chicken and pat dry. Add the chicken, onion, and tomatoes to the Dutch oven and toss everything together to coat evenly. Cover and cook for 45 to 55 minutes, until the juices run clear from a cut between the thigh and leg.

SNEAKY NOODLES

Serves 4

THOUGH MY KIDS HAVE FAIRLY sophisticated palates, if it were up to them they'd eat pasta every day. Sneaking some vegetables into the tomato sauce is a good way to fill them with added nutrition in the guise of their favorite dish. A tomato base can easily disguise zucchini, carrots, or any other vegetables you choose to put in.

3 tablespoons plus 2 teaspoons kosher salt

1 pound linguine

2 medium zucchini

2 carrots

2 medium tomatoes

1 medium yellow onion

Extra virgin olive oil

2 cups tomato-vegetable juice cocktail (V8 works perfectly for me)

Pinch of freshly ground black pepper

- Fill a large pot with 5 quarts of water, add 3 tablespoons of the salt, and bring to a boil. Add the pasta and cook until al dente. Drain and set aside.

- Meanwhile, grate the zucchini and carrots, lengthwise, with a fine grater. Grate the tomatoes and onion with a medium grater.

- Heat the olive oil in a large skillet. Add the grated vegetables and sauté over medium heat until tender, 5 to 7 minutes. Add the tomato-vegetable juice and season with the remaining 2 teaspoons salt and the pepper. Allow the juice to reduce for 5 minutes.

- Add the pasta to the skillet and coat thoroughly with the sauce. Serve.

ASPARAGUS

WITH

WILD WEST DRESSING

Serves 4, with about 1½ cups
dressing

PRETTY MUCH THE ONLY GREEN
vegetable my kids ask to eat is asparagus. I think the shape makes it fun for
them, as does the fact that they can
hold it in their hands. This ranch dressing seals the deal. It's tasty, of course,
and kids love to play with their food.
(And so do adults—isn't that what dip
is all about?)

WILD WEST DRESSING
1 garlic clove
1 teaspoon kosher salt, plus more to taste
¾ cup mayonnaise
⅓ cup sour cream
¼ cup buttermilk
½ teaspoon fresh lemon juice
3 tablespoons minced fresh chives
2 tablespoons minced fresh flat-leaf parsley
1 tablespoon minced fresh dill (optional)

Olive oil
1 bunch (about 1 pound) asparagus, ends trimmed
Kosher salt
Freshly ground black pepper

For the Dressing

- Using a fork, mash the garlic with the salt. The coarse texture of the salt will help turn the garlic into a mushy paste.
  Scrape this into a mixing bowl and add the mayonnaise, sour
  cream, buttermilk, and lemon juice. Stir really well and
  adjust the salt if needed.

- Throw in all the chopped herbs and stir the mixture once
  more. Store in an airtight container in the refrigerator until
  ready to use. The dressing will keep for about 1½ weeks, but
  at my house it's usually gone after a day.

For the Asparagus

- Preheat a cast-iron ridged grill pan over medium to high heat
  (if you don't have one, a regular skillet will do, but I prefer the
  ridged pan for the hot-off-the-grill illusion). Drizzle a little
  bit of olive oil into the pan and add the asparagus. Season with
  a little salt and pepper and cook for 3 to 5 minutes.

- I'll let you make the call on serving it either hot or cold, but
  never, ever forget to douse it in the Wild West Dressing. Your
  kids will love you for it.

RED VELVET GNOCCHI

Serves 6 to 8

WHEN I WORKED AT A WELL- known restaurant in Israel, my boss made me roll 4 pounds of gnocchi a day. I got so into it that I found myself singing Ramazzotti in the kitchen. This dish is much easier to make than traditional gnocchi—so simple that your kids can help. Gnocchi is typically made with potatoes, flour, and eggs, but I use semolina, milk, and beets instead. Beets are healthy (they're loaded with potassium) and add color.

2 cups whole milk
8 tablespoons (1 stick) unsalted butter
1½ cups semolina flour
2 tablespoons grated Parmesan, plus more for sprinkling
⅛ teaspoon grated nutmeg
2 tablespoons kosher salt
Pinch of freshly ground black pepper
1 to 2 small beets (about ½ pound), boiled until tender and cooled
2 large egg yolks
All-purpose flour for the work surface

- Combine the milk and 7 tablespoons of the butter in a large pot over medium heat until the butter is completely melted. Mix in the semolina flour and keep stirring until the mixture becomes thick and creamy, about 10 minutes. Remove from the heat and add the Parmesan, nutmeg, salt, and pepper. Stir well and cool completely.

- Peel the beets, cut off the stems, and puree the beets in a food processor until smooth. Add the egg yolks and mix just until well incorporated. Scrape the beet puree into the semolina dough and use your hands to combine all the ingredients thoroughly.

- Preheat the oven to 350°F. Line a baking sheet with parchment paper.

- Drop a scoop of dough onto a heavily floured surface and shape into a flat disk about 2 inches in diameter. Repeat until you run out of dough. Arrange the gnocchi in a single layer on the lined baking sheet. Melt the remaining tablespoon of butter and brush the tops of each gnocchi. Sprinkle the gnocchi with the Parmesan. Bake for 15 to 20 minutes.

ROOT VEGGIE CHIPS

Makes 6 to 8 cups

"MOM, I WANT A SNACK!"
Sure, you could just tear open a bag of chips. But if you think ahead on a day when you've got a bit of extra time, why not try a different approach? Baking beets, sweet potatoes, and turnips makes for delicious healthy chips.

You can also make this recipe with zucchini, summer squash, carrots, parsnips, and of course your run-of-the-mill potatoes. Taro makes a great chip too. Try experimenting with different spices like cayenne, garlic powder, or cumin. One of my nifty tricks is to use a salad mister to spritz the olive oil on the vegetable slices, which gives them a nice even coating.

1 beet
1 sweet potato
1 turnip
Extra virgin olive oil
Kosher salt
Oregano (optional)

- Preheat the oven to 225°F.

- Place an oven-safe cooling rack over a large baking sheet.

- Using a mandoline or a very sharp knife, slice each vegetable into paper-thin rounds and place side by side in a single layer on the rack. Drizzle on a little olive oil and bake just until the veggie chips are crisp and dry, 1 to 1½ hours. Toss with a little bit of salt and oregano.

POP, POP, POPCORN

I MEET SO MANY PEOPLE WHO'VE NEVER MADE THEIR OWN POPCORN, AND I always think they're missing out. I suppose I get it: given the availability of packaged and microwave-ready varieties, why bother making your own? But the fun you and your kids will have watching a pan full of kernels go *pop-pop-pop!*—and then mixing in the flavor of your choice—is priceless and creates wonderful family memories. Cover the pot with a splatter guard instead of a lid; this way you and the kids can watch the kernels explode before your very eyes, and you'll end up with a crisper product. Here are three varieties— two sweet, one savory.

COCONUTTY MILK CHOCOLATE

Makes about 6 cups

1 cup milk chocolate chips
3 tablespoons coconut milk
2 tablespoons canola oil
¼ cup popcorn kernels
2 tablespoons unsweetened coconut flakes

- Place the chocolate chips in a double boiler and heat until they are melted and smooth. Remove from the heat and stir in the coconut milk. Set aside.

- Line a large baking sheet with parchment paper.

- Heat the oil in a large pot. Drop one kernel into the pan and cover with an oil splatter guard. Once the kernel pops, the oil is ready. Add the remaining popcorn kernels, give the pan a quick shake, and cover. The popping should begin in about 30 seconds. Once it does, gently move the pan back and forth over the heat. When the popping slows down to a 2-second interval, remove from the heat and scatter the popcorn into a single layer on the lined baking sheet.

- Scrape the chocolate mixture into a large resealable plastic bag. Cut a teeny-tiny tip from the bottom corner of the bag and drizzle chocolate generously over the popcorn. Sprinkle on the coconut flakes and allow the chocolate to harden, about 20 minutes. If you're impatient like me, just pop the baking sheet into your refrigerator for 5 to 7 minutes; that should do the trick.

KETTLE CORN

Makes about 6 cups

2 tablespoons canola oil
¼ cup popcorn kernels
2 tablespoons unsalted butter
¼ cup sugar
Kosher salt

- Heat the oil in a large saucepan. Drop one kernel into the pan and cover with an oil splatter guard. Once the kernel pops, the oil is ready. Add the remaining popcorn kernels along with the butter and sugar. Give the pan a quick shake and cover. The popping should begin in about 30 seconds. Once it does, gently move the pan back and forth over the heat. When the popping slows down to a 2-second interval, remove from the heat and transfer to a large serving bowl. Add salt to taste.

GARLIC PARMESAN

Makes about 6 cups

3 tablespoons unsalted butter
1 garlic clove, pressed or finely chopped
1 cup grated Parmesan
Pinch of cayenne or more to taste
2 tablespoons canola oil
¼ cup popcorn kernels

- Combine the butter and garlic in a small saucepan and sauté briefly over low heat. Remove from heat and set aside.

- Combine the Parmesan and cayenne in a small bowl.

- Heat the oil in a large pot. Drop one kernel into the pan and cover with an oil splatter guard. Once the kernel pops, the oil is ready. Add the remaining popcorn kernels, give the pan a quick shake, and cover again. The popping should begin in about 30 seconds. Once it does, gently move the pan back and forth over the heat. When the popping slows down to a 2-second interval, remove from the heat and transfer to a large serving bowl.

- Dump the Parmesan and garlic mixtures over the popcorn and toss around to coat evenly.

BANANA DATE LIME SMOOTHIE

Makes about 2 cups

2 bananas, peeled and cut into 1-inch pieces
½ teaspoon freshly squeezed lime juice
5 to 6 dates, pitted
2 cups soy milk (or any other milk)
3 cups ice cubes

- Combine all the ingredients in a blender and puree until smooth. Easy-peasy.

WHEN I FIRST DREW UP THE beverage list for my falafel place, Taïm, I knew this smoothie would be a favorite. The combination of tastes, the natural sweetness of the dates, the drop of lime that cuts through the sweetness, and the soy milk that I can't consume except in this refreshing smoothie . . . need I say more?

MOJITO FRUIT SALAD

Serves 6 to 8

FOR ME, FRESH FRUIT CAN never be a dessert—I prefer chocolate. But once my big sister, Dorit, created this icy-cold fruit salad, I decided to compromise. When you use frozen fruit, you'll get an instant sauce; as the fruit thaws, it becomes perfect for slurping. I always love the way the juices melt from the frozen fruits and meld all the wonderful flavors together. Most important, kids love it. And that's what this chapter is all about!

One 16-ounce package frozen peaches
One 10-ounce package frozen mango
One 10-ounce package frozen strawberries
One 10-ounce package frozen blueberries
$\frac{1}{4}$ cup agave syrup
$\frac{1}{2}$ cup fresh mint leaves, coarsely chopped
Grated zest of 1 lemon
Juice of 1 lemon or orange

- Combine all the ingredients in a large serving bowl. Toss to coat evenly and cover with plastic wrap. Let the fruits thaw for 1 hour on your kitchen counter before serving.

HURRY, HURRY, HURRY!

QUICK
AND
EASY
MEALS

Like all Israelis,

I was drafted into the military when I was eighteen.

I REQUESTED A SPOT IN Armored, where I hoped to be a firing instructor on the $60-million Merkava battle tank—the most elite job open to women at the time. But after reviewing my high school transcript (Cs and Ds) and psychological profile (I can only guess), the army instead assigned me to the Nevatim Air Base, where I'd serve as a chauffeur for fighter pilots.

As a driver, I sat at the bottom of air force hierarchy—lower even than the team of high school dropouts who painted white lines on the runway. While air force pilots were considered the cream of the crop, we drivers certainly were not. But I soon discovered that air force life had its perks. Fridays, when soldiers across Israel rode public buses home for the Sabbath, I flew to Tel Aviv by helicopter. My base had a swimming pool—not that I was allowed to use it often, but still.

And then there was the food.

On most army bases, eighteen-year-old enlisted cooks prepared industrial quantities of hard-boiled eggs, cottage cheese, and toast for breakfast and dinner and hot dog stew for lunch. But because such ordinary fare wasn't good enough for Israel's chosen ones, the air force bused in a pair of elderly Yemenite women from the nearby town of Arad to prepare home-cooked meals for the elite pilots.

The Yemenite grandmothers in the pilots' kitchen cooked like my mother did: a pinch of cumin here, a pinch of paprika there. No cookbooks, no recipes.

Just their intuition. I began to spend time with them, and soon they asked me to help out. I prepared side dishes to accompany their grilled chicken and spiced beef. Whatever instinct inspired them guided me as well.

Eventually they promoted me from appetizers to main courses. Most days we worked as a trio; on others I cooked alone while they relaxed. As we cooked, the old women and I gossiped and told stories. They became my surrogate mothers, the kitchen at Nevatim my new home away from home.

I intended to keep my new hobby a secret, but somehow my commanding officer found out. Miraculously, he allowed me to continue to moonlight in the kitchen, so long as it didn't interfere with my duties as a driver.

Conditions in the pilots' kitchen were less than ideal. The spatulas were cracked, the pots rusted. I was limited to basic ingredients—fighter jocks or not, Nevatim was still a military base that operated on a military budget. And I had little time: because I was first and foremost a driver, I could be paged away from the kitchen at any moment for a pilot pickup. I cooked at a furious pace lest I get called out to the runway before my bread had time to rise or my chicken had fully roasted.

On an overcast morning in January 1991, the Israel Defense Forces chiefs of staff convened at Nevatim to plot strategy. The United States was preparing to bomb Iraq; the Israeli generals feared Saddam Hussein would retaliate with an attack on Israel. The Jewish state faced nothing less than an existential challenge, but the Nevatim Air Base faced an even larger one:

The chiefs of staff would be staying for dinner.

The commanding officer of the 116th Air Division summoned me to his office. "Cook the generals a feast," he ordered. He gave me three hours to do it.

I rounded up my two favorite fighter pilots and made them sous-chefs for the night. I then raided the enlisted soldiers' mess hall pantry for the chicken, soy, Persian rice, ginger, and zucchini I'd need for the Chinese-themed banquet I envisioned.

I don't remember much from that night, but a few details stand out: the parade of generals, many of whom I recognized from television, as they filed into the pilots' dining hall; crouching in the corner of the kitchen as I prayed to a god to whom I hadn't spoken since elementary school that the generals might find no fault in my meal or—miracle of miracles—enjoy it; and the standing ovation I received after the commanding officer of the 116th Air Wing summoned me into the dining hall.

Sometimes a quick meal is as satisfying as one that has been carefully planned out. These recipes are easy to make—between preparation and cooking, each dish takes less than thirty minutes.

Perfect for when you have your own little army to feed.

SHAKSHUKA

Serves 4 to 6

IN ISRAEL THE WORD *SHAK-shuka* is synonymous with breakfast. It's best with a slice or two of challah bread to sop up the juices. This is a version of my dad's recipe, except that he used to mix the eggs together, because my older sister refused to eat the egg whites. Here is the recipe I prefer.

3 tablespoons canola oil
2 medium yellow onions, chopped
1 large green bell pepper, cored, seeded, and chopped
1 large jalapeño chile, cored, seeded, and chopped
7 garlic cloves, finely chopped
¼ cup tomato paste
One 28-ounce can whole peeled tomatoes, crushed by hand
1 bay leaf
2½ tablespoons sugar
1½ tablespoons kosher salt
1 tablespoon sweet Hungarian paprika
1 tablespoon ground cumin
1½ teaspoons freshly ground black pepper
1 teaspoon ground caraway
½ bunch Swiss chard, stemmed and chopped, or spinach
8 to 12 large eggs

- Heat the oil in a large skillet. Add the onions and sauté over medium heat until translucent, 5 to 10 minutes. Add the bell peppers and jalapeño and cook just until softened, 3 to 5 minutes. Stir in the garlic and tomato paste and sauté for another 2 minutes.

- Slowly pour in the tomatoes. Stir in the bay leaf, sugar, salt, paprika, cumin, pepper, and caraway and let the mixture simmer for 20 minutes. Layer the Swiss chard leaves on top.

- Crack the eggs into the tomato mixture. Cover and simmer for approximately 10 minutes or until the whites of the eggs are no longer translucent.

EIGHTEEN-MINUTE RICE

Serves 4

MY MOTHER'S PERSIAN RICE is terrific, but it takes more than an hour to make, so I use this shortcut version when time is limited. I first learned this recipe in culinary school, and I remember thinking how upset my mother would be if she knew I was cutting corners. I use jasmine rice because it's less starchy than sushi rice and less dry than basmati. There are endless ways to prepare this rice. Go wild.

2 tablespoons canola oil

2 cups jasmine rice, rinsed and drained

1½ tablespoons kosher salt

- Heat the oil in a 3-quart saucepan over medium heat, add the rice and salt, and sauté for 3 minutes (see Note).

- Meanwhile, bring 3 cups water to a boil in a small saucepan.

- Slowly, very slowly add the boiling water to the rice. Be careful, because it will start to bubble like hot lava. Give the rice a quick stir and lower the heat just until the rice is simmering. Cover with a lid and cook for 18 minutes. Turn off the heat and leave the lid on for another 3 minutes.

- Okay, so it's not exactly 18 minutes, but it's pretty darn close.

Note: For a quick infusion of flavor, while you are sautéing the rice, throw in a cinnamon stick and a bay leaf, or cumin seeds, or some caramelized onions.

SPICY-ISH FISH

Serves 4

WITH MY FATHER'S PERFECT hot sauce, called *s'chug,* and just two more ingredients, you're about to prepare a spicy fish that, thanks to the coconut milk, has the flavor of Thailand. For best results, serve with wedges of fresh lime to lighten up the richness of the coconut milk.

1½ cups coconut milk

½ cup vegetable stock (or pineapple juice if you're feeling a bit daring)

2 tablespoons S'chug (page 275)

Four 6-ounce white fish fillets (snapper, tilapia, bass, or grouper)

Fresh cilantro

Lime or lemon wedges

- Whisk together the coconut milk, vegetable stock, and *s'chug* in a large skillet, over medium heat. Bring the mixture to a simmer, then add the fish fillets, cover, and cook until the fish is milky white, 6 to 8 minutes—this will depend on the texture of the fish. Remove from the heat, garnish with a handful of cilantro and some lime wedges, and serve right from the skillet.

ROASTED BROCCOLI

Serves 4 to 6

PEOPLE ALWAYS UNDER-estimate this vegetable, so I'm hoping the preparation you find here will change your mind forever. Broccoli is usually boiled or steamed—and the result can be mushy. Roasting it preserves the crispness. A simple vinaigrette can be added at the end.

2 pounds broccoli
8 to 12 garlic cloves, unpeeled
⅓ cup extra virgin olive oil
½ teaspoon kosher salt
¼ teaspoon freshly ground black pepper
Grated zest of 1 lemon
Juice of ½ lemon

- Preheat the oven to 400°F. Line a large baking sheet with parchment paper and set aside.

- Trim the broccoli into bite-sized florets and place the broccoli in a mixing bowl. Add the garlic cloves, olive oil, salt, pepper, lemon zest, and lemon juice and toss to combine thoroughly.

- Arrange the broccoli in a single layer on the lined baking sheet. Roast in the oven until crisp-tender and parts of the florets have developed a nice brown color, 20 to 30 minutes.

PATATAS BRAVAS

Serves 4

I HAVE ALWAYS THOUGHT OF this as a Spanish version of french fries. It's served as tapas in bars throughout Spain; here I serve it with za'atar and roasted garlic aioli. Za'atar is an actual herb, but when people say "za'atar" they're most likely referring to a blend of dry sumac, sesame seeds, and salt.

5 cups canola oil
4 large russet potatoes, peeled and cut into 1-inch cubes
Kosher salt
Za'atar seasoning (see Note)
Garlic Aioli (page 268)

- Heat the oil in a large, heavy pot until the temperature reaches 350°F.

- With a slotted spoon, drop some of the potato cubes into the hot oil and fry until tender and golden brown, 15 to 20 minutes. Remove with your slotted spoon and drain on a few sheets of paper towel. Repeat until all the potatoes are fried.

- Place the potatoes in a large bowl and sprinkle with salt and za'atar seasoning. Serve immediately with a side of my famous aioli.

Note: If you can't find za'atar in a Middle Eastern market, a mixture of dried oregano and sesame seeds is an acceptable substitute.

ZUCCHINI PATTIES

Serves 4 to 6

THIS DISH IS SO INCREDIBLY simple to make, but the results are exquisite. Serve with plain yogurt or, better, with the same Wild West Dressing you made for the kids (page 59). In a pinch, bread crumbs from store-bought challah are fine too.

12/30/13: Didn't cohere at all

3 medium zucchini
1 medium yellow onion
1 leek, white and light green parts only, finely chopped
2½ tablespoons finely chopped fresh dill
⅓ cup crumbs made from Challah (page 24)
1 large egg, beaten
Canola oil
Kosher salt

- Finely grate the zucchini and onion. Wrap the grated vegetables in a clean dish towel and twist both ends over the kitchen sink to squeeze out all the excess moisture.

- Combine the zucchini, onion, leek, dill, and bread crumbs in a large bowl. Add the egg and use your hands to mix everything together. Shape the mixture into 2-inch patties.

- Add ½ inch of oil to a large skillet and heat over medium heat. Cook the zucchini patties in the hot oil until both sides are golden brown, 3 to 5 minutes. Drain on paper towels and season with salt.

SHRIMP, SPANISH STYLE

Serves 4

WHEN I DREAM OF SEAFOOD, I drift off to Barcelona. There really is no better place for fresh fish—it's simply divine. When I spent time there, I'd sit at Bar Central inside the Boqueria and wouldn't leave my seat until I tried the entire day's menu.

This shrimp dish is delicious, fast, and easy to prepare. Use the best olive oil you can get your hands on, so you can enjoy the oily sauce—in the end, you'll love to soak it up with any extra bread. I like my shrimp spicy, but feel free to play around with the proportions, so long as you don't overcook it.

$3/4$ **pound tiger shrimp (about 16 pieces), peeled and deveined, tails intact**
2 teaspoons kosher salt
$1/4$ **teaspoon freshly ground black pepper**
$2/3$ **cup extra virgin olive oil**
2 to 3 garlic cloves, thinly sliced
9 small dried red chiles or $1/4$ teaspoon chile flakes
3 to 4 Perfect Preserved Lemons (page 276), sliced
Fresh parsley or cilantro, chopped
Crusty bread for serving

- Season the shrimp with the salt and pepper and set aside.

- Combine the olive oil, garlic, and red chiles in a cold skillet. Sauté over very low heat (so the garlic doesn't burn) for about 5 minutes, to really infuse the oil. Add the preserved lemons.

- Crank up the heat to high, add the shrimp, and cook until just opaque, about 1 minute on each side. Remove from the heat, transfer to a serving dish, olive oil included, and add a sprinkling of parsley or cilantro. Don't forget to serve it with a side of crusty bread to sop up all the garlicky goodness.

MUSSELS DRENCHED

I N

OUZO

Serves 4

ONE OF MY FAVORITE MEMORIES is sitting on my in-laws' patio in Provence, on a sweltering summer day, drinking pastis—a licorice-flavored drink. I loved the French atmosphere, not the drink, which is too strong for me. But I found a way to bury the licorice flavor—mussels! And that led me to devise this recipe, which uses ouzo, a liquor more appropriate to Middle Eastern cooking, instead of pastis.

Use pastis or Pernod if you can't find ouzo.

2 tablespoons extra virgin olive oil
2 tablespoons unsalted butter
4 garlic cloves, thinly sliced
1 cup chopped shallots
$\frac{1}{2}$ pint cherry tomatoes, halved lengthwise
$\frac{1}{2}$ fennel bulb, cored and thinly sliced
2 teaspoons kosher salt
$\frac{1}{4}$ teaspoon freshly ground black pepper
$\frac{1}{4}$ teaspoon chile flakes
2 teaspoons chopped fresh thyme
$\frac{1}{2}$ cup ouzo
$\frac{1}{2}$ cup dry white wine
2 pounds mussels, cleaned and debearded
2 tablespoons chopped fresh parsley
2 tablespoons chopped fennel fronds
Crusty baguette for dipping

- Heat the olive oil and butter in a large pot over low heat, add the garlic, and sauté for 2 minutes. Add the shallots, turn up the heat to medium, and sauté just until translucent, about 5 minutes. Add the cherry tomatoes and fennel bulb. Mix in the salt, pepper, chile flakes, and thyme and sauté for another 3 minutes.

- Add the ouzo and wine to the pot and reduce for 5 minutes. Throw in the mussels and cover with a lid. The mussels are ready once all the shells have opened up, 7 to 10 minutes. Remove from the heat and toss in the parsley and fennel fronds. Using two large spoons, toss the mussels around with the ouzo juices.

- I usually go the lazy route and take the entire pot right to the table, but you can put it in a large serving bowl if you prefer. Serve with the bread and never, ever eat the mussels that didn't open—it's a recipe for disaster.

YOU'VE BEEN CHOPPED

Serves 4 to 6

THIS SALAD IS BASICALLY A
collection of random ingredients,
inspired by memories of my days working at the Spanish restaurant Bolo in
New York, where they had what is probably the best chopped salad on the
planet. Of course when there's a little
more time, fresh corn and freshly
cooked black beans are better, but
sometimes my grumbling stomach
tells me otherwise.

LIME VINAIGRETTE
3 tablespoons olive oil
1 tablespoon fresh lime juice
¼ teaspoon kosher salt
Pinch of freshly ground black pepper
Pinch of sugar

SALAD
**5 or 6 fistfuls baby spinach, sliced into thin strips
(julienned, if you're fancy)**
1 cup drained canned corn kernels
1 cup drained and rinsed canned black beans
**1 small red bell pepper, cored, seeded, and cut into small
cubes (about 1 cup)**
⅓ cup store-bought crispy shallots or fried onions
1 small avocado, cut into small cubes
1 jalapeño chile, cored, seeded, and cut into small cubes
3 tablespoons finely chopped fresh cilantro or basil

- Slowly whisk the olive oil into the lime juice. Then add the
salt, pepper, and sugar. Toss all the salad ingredients together
with the lime vinaigrette. It doesn't get any easier than this!

AUNT CHANA'S TOMATO SALAD

Serves 4

MY AUNT CHANA CAN WHIP UP a bowl of tomato salad in under three minutes. I've always loved her version—so much that I'd drink the juices from the plate when no one was watching. I add basil for an Italian flair, but you can try cilantro or mint instead. For an aesthetic change, try heirloom tomatoes when they're in season.

5 large tomatoes (any variety will do)
1 small yellow onion, thinly sliced
½ cup fresh basil or mint, chopped
⅓ cup white wine vinegar
2½ teaspoons sugar
1 tablespoon kosher salt
Extra virgin olive oil

- Cut the tomatoes into wedges and place in a serving dish along with the onion and basil.

- Whisk together the vinegar, sugar, and salt in a small bowl. Pour the dressing over the tomato salad and toss lightly to coat. Drizzle the olive oil over the salad right before serving.

LINGUINE

WITH

ROASTED PEPPERS

AND

KALAMATA OLIVES

Serves 4

BEFORE I STARTED CULINARY school, I worked as a waitress in a coffee shop called Kapulski, which is pretty much the Starbucks of Israel except that (a) they have a full food menu, and (b) they don't pay nearly as well as Starbucks pays its baristas. Anyway, it wasn't exactly a job to brag about. But learning to prepare Kapulski's red pepper Kalamata linguine made me fall in love with cooking. If you happen to have fresh pasta on hand, this dish is even better! And if you're not in so much of a hurry, using homemade roasted bell peppers takes this dish to another level.

Kosher salt
1 pound dried linguine
3 tablespoons olive oil
1 medium red onion, thinly sliced
4 garlic cloves, thinly sliced
1 cup thinly sliced store-bought roasted bell peppers
¾ cup Kalamata olives, pitted and halved
2 teaspoons soy sauce
1 teaspoon sugar
Pinch of freshly ground black pepper
¼ teaspoon chile flakes

- Fill a large pot with water and add salt until it tastes like the ocean. Bring the water to a boil. Add the pasta and cook just until al dente, 8 to 10 minutes (3 minutes for fresh).

- Meanwhile, heat the olive oil in a large skillet over medium heat. Add the onion and sauté until translucent, 5 to 7 minutes. Add the garlic and cook until a light golden brown color, 2 to 3 minutes. Add the roasted peppers and olives and sauté for another 3 minutes.

- In a small bowl, whisk together the soy sauce, sugar, 1 teaspoon salt, the pepper, and the chile flakes. Pour the sauce into the skillet and cook together for 3 minutes. Lower the heat to a simmer.

- Drain the pasta, but reserve about ½ cup of the cooking liquid. Add the linguine and reserved cooking liquid to the skillet and toss together with the sauce. Remove from the heat and serve immediately.

THE FIRST CUT IS THE DEEPEST

FOODS THAT COMFORT

For me, food is all about memory.

Which is why my ultimate comfort food is a piping-hot *sufganiya*—a jelly doughnut.

IT ALL GOES BACK TO MY second year of high school, when my heart was broken by a short, gluten-free boy named Yonatan.

I was not alone in my passion for Yonatan. Despite his acne and braces, and the celiac disease that caused his belly to swell like a beach ball at the mere scent of pita, he was full of charm and warmth and had a stranglehold on the heart of every girl in the tenth grade. And somehow, from among the masses, he chose me.

Our love was all consuming in the way that only teenage love can be. He was my first crush and my first kiss. He was also my first chance to express my love for another person through cooking. At this point I was really beginning to get serious in the kitchen. And with Yonatan's celiac condition, I'd discovered a way to shower him with love in a way no one else could.

Thursday afternoons, I'd rush home and bake him *jahnun,* the traditional Yemenite rolled dough eaten on the Sabbath, made with potato flour. One Friday night I walked three miles to his house on the other side of Ramat Gan (there were no buses since it was the Sabbath), carrying a ribbon-adorned pastry box filled with three dozen gluten-free chocolate chip cookies in my hand. I felt such pride as I marched down Ben Gurion Street, the pastry box in my hand like a trophy.

For eighteen months, Yonatan was my world. Then, one rainy December afternoon, he called to say it was over.

"Wha— What do you mean?" I stammered.

I ran to his house (there were buses this time, but how could I possibly wait around for a bus?), certain that if he could just see me in person he'd change his mind.

No dice. He had met someone else, and he wanted her. Not me.

I walked home in the steady drizzle, raindrops mixing with my tears. I was crushed, but more than that I simply didn't understand. How could such true love die? He'd written me poetry. Lots of poetry. He'd made me a mix tape, goddammit, a *mix tape*! How could such pure love be over?

Back home, I sat myself down at the kitchen table in front of a freshly baked batch of *sufganiyot*—the traditional doughnuts that Israelis eat on Hanukkah.

I dove into that platter of doughnuts as if I hadn't eaten in a year. And in a way I hadn't: for eighteen months, I'd been faithful to Yonatan not only in my heart but also through my diet. If my true love could not eat pita, pizza, or ice cream cones, then neither would I! But now, with Yonatan out of the picture, there was no need to be chaste.

I ravaged three, four jelly doughnuts in a row, the jelly spurting hot inside my cheeks and dribbling off my chin. Revenge is always sweet, but all the more so when it's filled with jelly.

Now and forevermore, whenever I eat a jelly doughnut, I'm transported back to that December afternoon at my kitchen table. It was a moment in which I felt my troubles disappear.

And isn't this what comfort food is all about?

Here are recipes for some of my favorite cheer-me-up dishes. Obviously, it's a totally subjective list. It's eclectic too, the one common trait of these dishes being that for the most part they're hot foods. This isn't coincidental; I turn to hot foods for comfort because they can't be gobbled down. The heat forces me to eat slowly and, in the process, pull back from the world and whatever's got me feeling down.

MY MOM'S RICE STEW

Serves 4 to 6

THIS JUST MIGHT BE THE MOST
special recipe in this entire book—not
because it's particularly tricky or
tastes better than the rest, but because
it's a reflection of my changing relationship with my mother, from anger
to rebellion to acceptance and, finally,
love. When my mom makes this stew,
she uses chicken neck. I happen to love
the texture and taste, but I'll spare
you—I've suggested chicken wings
instead. This recipe also uses black-
eyed peas, but you can try adding
chickpeas for a completely different
experience.

1 cup Arborio rice
1½ cups dried black-eyed peas
Kosher salt
¼ cup Pomegranate Confiture (page 273) or pomegranate molasses
2 tablespoons sugar
2 tablespoons canola oil
1 pound chicken wings
7 pitted prunes, cut into thirds
2 dried Persian limes, halved
1 teaspoon ground cumin
½ teaspoon freshly ground black pepper
4 cups chicken stock or vegetable stock
4 cups water
2 bay leaves

• Soak the rice in cold water for 20 minutes, then drain. While the rice is soaking, boil the black-eyed peas in salted water for 30 minutes. Discard the cooking liquid and reserve the black-eyed peas until ready to use.

• Mix together the pomegranate confiture and sugar and set aside.

• Heat the canola oil in a large pot over medium-high heat. Season the chicken wings with 1 tablespoon salt and add them to the hot oil. Sauté until golden brown on all sides, about 7 minutes. Add the prunes and Persian limes and sauté for another 3 minutes. Stir in the black-eyed peas, then sea-son with the cumin, 2 tablespoons salt, and pepper.

• Pour in the chicken stock, water, and pomegranate confi-ture mixture and stir well. Throw in the bay leaves and simmer for 15 minutes.

• Add the rice and simmer over low heat for 1 hour, stirring frequently. The stew is ready when the meat is nearly fall-ing off the bone and most of the liquid has been absorbed by the rice.

LENTIL FETA SALAD

Serves 4 to 6

LENTILS ARE CHEAP, NUTRI-tious, and easy to work with. I find them to be a total comfort food. I like them warm in the winter—but here I make a cold dish mixed with spinach and feta, which lighten it up.

LENTILS
3/4 cup dried lentils
1 1/4 cups grated carrots
1 medium shallot, finely chopped (about 1/4 cup)
1 bay leaf
1 cup water
1 tablespoon kosher salt

DRESSING
2 tablespoons white balsamic vinegar
1 tablespoon finely chopped shallot
1/4 cup canola oil
2 teaspoons kosher salt
Pinch of freshly ground black pepper

SALAD
6 cups spinach
1/3 cup crumbled feta
Roasted bell peppers (optional)

For the Lentils

- Combine the ingredients in a medium saucepan and bring to a boil. Lower the heat to simmer and cook until the lentils are tender, about 40 minutes. Remove from the heat and discard the cooking liquid and bay leaf. Cool completely before mixing with the salad.

For the Dressing

- Combine the vinegar and shallot in a food processor and puree until well blended. Slowly drizzle in the canola oil with the motor running, until thickened. Season the vinaigrette with the salt and pepper to taste.

For the Salad

- In a large salad bowl, toss together the spinach, feta, and cooked lentils. Add the vinaigrette to taste and, if desired, some roasted bell peppers.

CHAMUSTA

Serves 4 to 6

LIKE A FEW OTHER RECIPES in this book, I owe this one to my friend Guy. If I get mad at Guy, all I need to do is eat his amazing *chamusta,* and I soon forget why I was upset. *Chamusta* is a Kurdish sour soup that's traditionally served with a semolina dumpling stuffed with minced meat. My recipe turns the dumpling inside out, creating a meatball with semolina inside. *Baharat* is an Israeli spice blend; make my version or look for it in ethnic markets.

3 tablespoons extra virgin olive oil

7 garlic cloves, coarsely chopped

2 celery ribs, coarsely chopped

1 leek, white and light green parts only, thinly sliced

½ bunch Swiss chard (about 2½ cups), coarsely chopped

1 cup fresh lemon juice (from 4 to 6 lemons)

6 cups chicken stock

¾ teaspoon ground turmeric

1 tablespoon sugar

Kosher salt

Freshly ground black pepper

KEBAB

1 pound ground beef

½ cup semolina flour

1 medium yellow onion, grated

2 cloves Roasted Garlic (page 273), finely chopped

½ cup finely chopped parsley

1 teaspoon Baharat (page 264)

1 teaspoon ground cumin

1 teaspoon sweet Hungarian paprika

½ teaspoon chile flakes

2 teaspoons kosher salt

¼ teaspoon freshly ground black pepper

2 tablespoons canola oil

- Heat the olive oil in a large pot over medium heat and add the garlic, celery, and leek. Sauté until tender, about 5 minutes. Add the Swiss chard and sauté for another 3 minutes. Add the lemon juice and chicken stock. Stir in the turmeric and sugar and add salt and pepper to taste. Bring to a boil, then lower the heat to simmer and cook for 45 minutes.

- Meanwhile, make the kebabs: Combine all the ingredients except the canola oil in a large bowl and roll the meat mixture into kebabs the size and shape of your thumb (you should be able to make about 16).

- Heat a large skillet (preferably cast iron) over high heat for 5 minutes, then add the canola oil. Grill the kebabs for 3 minutes on each side.

- To serve, put the kebabs at the bottom of a shallow bowl and top with a few ladles of *chamusta.*

NOT-SO-JEWISH CHICKEN SOUP

Serves 4 to 6

I'VE ALWAYS WONDERED JUST what it is about chicken soup that makes it the perfect cure for the common cold. Is it scientific fact or just a myth that's held on for generations? I think it all comes down to the power of belief. So if this chicken soup makes you feel better—and I believe it will—who cares about statistics and scientific truisms? You can add barley, noodles, or rice (or all three!) to give your body a boost of calories. My recipe also includes chorizo, which imparts a smoky flavor (and makes it not so Jewish). If you don't eat chorizo, merguez sausage works well too.

3 tablespoons canola oil

1 medium yellow onion, finely chopped (about 2 cups)

1½ leeks, white parts only, finely chopped

1 cup finely chopped celery

¾ cup coarsely chopped dried chorizo

1½ cups finely chopped carrots

1 bay leaf

2 thyme sprigs

1 pound chicken pieces with skin and bone, preferably dark meat

½ cup dry white wine

¼ cup plus 1 teaspoon kosher salt

⅛ teaspoon freshly ground black pepper

1 tablespoon ground cumin

1 teaspoon ground turmeric

12 cups water

1½ cups ½-inch cubes butternut squash

2 medium potatoes, cut into ½-inch cubes

- Heat the canola oil in a large pot over medium heat and add the onion, leeks, celery, and chorizo. Sauté for 10 minutes. Add the carrots, bay leaf, thyme, and chicken and sauté for another 10 minutes. Add the white wine and reduce to ¼ cup, 3 to 5 minutes.

- Stir in the salt, pepper, cumin, and turmeric. Sauté for 3 minutes and pour in the water. Bring to a boil and add the butternut squash and potatoes. Lower the heat and simmer for 40 minutes.

SINAYA

Serves 4 to 6

THIS IS A PALESTINIAN ARAB
dish that will rock your world. If you
can get your hands on a terra-cotta
dish, use it to prepare and serve the
sinaya in. Layer in the tomato, the fried
eggplant, the ground beef that's mixed
with spices and pine nuts, and finally
a thick helping of tahini—then slide it
all into the oven until the tahini
becomes crusty. This is Palestinian
comfort food at its best.

1 large eggplant
Kosher salt

TAHINI SAUCE
¾ cup tahini
⅓ cup fresh lemon juice
1 cup water
1 tablespoon olive oil
3 garlic cloves
1 tablespoon kosher salt

5 tablespoons extra virgin olive oil
2 large tomatoes, thinly sliced
1 medium yellow onion, finely chopped
5 garlic cloves, finely chopped
1 tablespoon tomato paste
1 pound ground beef
1 pound ground lamb
2 teaspoons Baharat (page 264)
2 teaspoons sweet Hungarian paprika
1 teaspoon ground cumin
¼ teaspoon freshly ground black pepper
⅓ cup finely chopped fresh parsley
1 tablespoon toasted pine nuts
1 loaf crusty bread

- Cut the eggplant into ¼-inch-thick slices and sprinkle
  with salt. Let it sit for 1 hour to allow the excess moisture
  to drip off.

- Preheat the oven to 375°F.

- Combine all the ingredients for the tahini sauce in a food
  processor and blend until smooth and creamy. Set aside until
  ready to use.

- Place the eggplant slices in a large baking dish and drizzle
  with 2 tablespoons of the olive oil. Bake in the oven for
  45 minutes. Remove from the oven and place the tomato
  slices on top of the eggplant. Set the baking dish aside but
  keep the oven on.

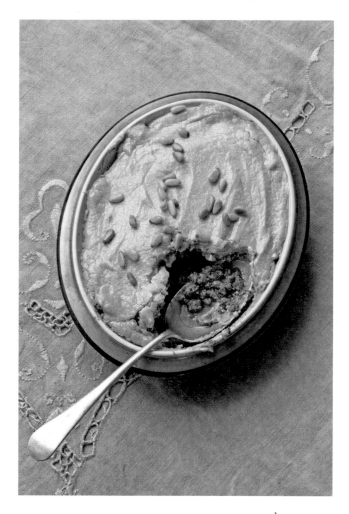

- Heat the remaining 3 tablespoons of olive oil in a large skillet over medium heat and add the onion. Sauté until translucent, about 5 minutes. Add the garlic and tomato paste and cook for another 5 minutes. Add the ground beef and lamb and season with the *baharat,* paprika, cumin, 2 teaspoons salt, and the pepper. Cook for another 20 minutes.

- Remove from the heat and stir in the parsley. Drain off the excess liquid and transfer the ground meat to the baking dish with the eggplant and tomato slices. Spread a generous layer of tahini sauce on the top, about $1/4$ inch thick. Bake in the oven until golden brown, about 30 minutes.

- Garnish with the pine nuts and serve with a side of crusty bread.

TURKEY BALLS

W I T H

OKRA

Serves 4 to 6

THERE ARE THREE KEY BENE- fits to this recipe: (1) Turkey is a healthy alternative to red meat. (2) The addition of challah bread makes for fluffier meatballs. (3) This will make you a convert to okra if you're not already a fan.

Serve on top of rice.

TURKEY BALLS

1 pound ground turkey

1½ tablespoons canola oil

1 teaspoon sweet Hungarian paprika

1½ teaspoons ground cumin

3 tablespoons kosher salt

½ teaspoon freshly ground black pepper

½ cup finely chopped fresh parsley

¼ cup finely chopped fresh cilantro

½ cup crumbs made from Challah (page 24)

OKRA SAUCE

3 tablespoons olive oil

1 medium yellow onion, finely chopped

1 pound okra, frozen or fresh, cut into thirds

1½ tablespoons tomato paste

4 plum tomatoes, finely chopped

¼ cup fresh lemon juice

1 teaspoon coriander seeds, crushed

1½ teaspoons sweet Hungarian paprika

½ teaspoon chile flakes

2 teaspoons sugar

1 tablespoon kosher salt

1 teaspoon freshly ground black pepper

For the Turkey Balls

- Combine all the ingredients in a large bowl and mix thoroughly. Make golf-ball-sized turkey balls and set aside until ready to use.

For the Okra Sauce and to Finish

- Heat the oil in a deep skillet over medium heat, add the onion, and sauté until translucent, about 5 minutes. Add the okra and cook for 5 minutes. Add the tomato paste and sauté for another 3 minutes. Add the chopped tomatoes and the lemon juice. Stir in the coriander, paprika, chile flakes, sugar, salt, and pepper.

- Bring the mixture to a boil and throw in the turkey balls. Bring to a boil again, then lower the heat to produce a rapid simmer. Cover with a lid and cook for 40 minutes, stirring occasionally.

SIMPLE BEANS

Serves 4

THIS IS ONE OF THOSE RECIPES you'll likely keep forever. It's simple, fast (literally, 10 minutes), and full of flavor. It's the perfect rainy-day healthy snack when you don't want to leave your couch and blanket for too long. The anchovy is key here, providing most of the flavor.

Kosher salt
½ pound green beans, trimmed
2 tablespoons unsalted butter
6 garlic cloves, thinly sliced
5 anchovy fillets
¼ teaspoon chile flakes
Lemon wedges

- Bring a medium pot of salted water to a boil and have a bowl of ice and water ready. Add the green beans and cook for 2 minutes, then dunk them into the ice bath. Allow the beans to cool completely, then drain them in a colander.

- Melt the butter in a skillet over medium heat, add the garlic, reduce the heat to low, and sauté until golden brown but not burned, about 3 minutes. Add the anchovies and sauté over low heat until the fillets begin to dissolve into the butter, about 3 minutes. Season with 2 teaspoons salt, add the chile flakes and green beans, and cook just until the beans are tender but still crispy, about 3 minutes. Serve with lemon wedges.

CREAMY, CHEESY POTATOES

Serves 4 to 6

THE POTATO IS PROBABLY THE one vegetable we could never live without. We all relate to french fries, mashed potatoes, and shepherd's pie; my husband loves vichyssoise (classic French leek-potato soup); and I believe our lives would be woefully different without it. This recipe is a little on the heavy side. You should experiment with different cheeses or mix a few together.

1 cup heavy cream

2 cups grated Parmesan (Gouda and Piave are great substitutes, or try a mix of all three)

½ cup ricotta

2 tablespoons finely chopped fresh thyme

1 tablespoon finely chopped fresh rosemary

1 tablespoon kosher salt

¼ teaspoon grated nutmeg

4 large russet potatoes, peeled and thinly sliced

2 tablespoons unsalted butter, melted

- Preheat the oven to 375°F.

- Mix together the cream, Parmesan, ricotta, thyme, rosemary, salt, and nutmeg in a large bowl. Toss in the sliced potatoes and coat thoroughly with the cream mixture.

- Scrape the contents into an ovenproof dish that's about 2 inches deep and drizzle the melted butter on top. Cover with aluminum foil and bake for 30 minutes. Remove the foil, crank up the oven heat to 425°F, and cook until brown and crispy on top, about 20 minutes.

SUFGANIYOT

Makes 15 to 20 doughnuts

A *SUFGANIYA* IS AN ISRAELI treat similar to a doughnut, but without the hole in the middle. The pastry is also stuffed with berry preserves and then topped with powdered sugar; you'll be left with sticky hands. We eat these delicacies at Hanukkah, when it's cold and rainy. You can experiment with your own fillings—I suggest peanut butter, chocolate, and dulce de leche to start.

3 cups all-purpose flour, plus flour for the work surface and baking sheet

$^3/_4$ cup whole milk, at room temperature

2 tablespoons active dry yeast

$^1/_3$ cup sugar, plus sugar for dusting

2 large eggs

2 teaspoons kosher salt

1 tablespoon brandy

2 tablespoons unsalted butter, at room temperature

Grated zest of $^1/_2$ lemon

Canola oil for deep frying and for the bowl

Blueberry or raspberry preserves

- Place the 3 cups flour in the large mixing bowl of a stand mixer; if you don't have a stand mixer, use a large mixing bowl. Create a large well in the center and pour in $^1/_4$ cup of the milk, the yeast, and 1 teaspoon of sugar. Let stand until the yeast mixture becomes foamy, about 10 minutes.

- In another bowl, stir the remaining $^1/_2$ cup milk, the remaining sugar, the eggs, salt, brandy, butter, and lemon zest.

- *If using a stand mixer:* With the dough hook attached, turn the mixer to low speed and mix the yeast mixture into the flour. Then slowly add the milk mixture, beating until just well combined, about 3 minutes. Crank up the setting to knead the dough for 5 minutes.

- *If using a mixing bowl:* Incorporate the flour with the yeast mixture using your hands. Then slowly pour in the milk mixture with one hand while working the flour into the liquid with the other. You can knead the mixture in the bowl or dump it on your kitchen counter over a lightly floured surface. Knead for 5 minutes.

- Shape the dough into a large ball and transfer to another bowl slicked with canola oil. Cover with plastic wrap and allow the dough to rise in a warm place away from any drafts. After an hour, the dough should double in size.

- Lightly flour the surface of your work area and roll the dough to a $^1/_4$-inch thickness. Use a $2^1/_2$-inch round cutter or drinking glass to cut the *sufganiyot* and place them on a lightly dusted baking sheet. Sprinkle a little flour on top of the *suf-*

ganiyot to prevent sticking and cover with plastic wrap. Let them rise for another 15 minutes in a warm place.

- Meanwhile, heat a deep skillet with 2 inches of oil to 365°F. Working in small batches, fry the *sufganiyot* in the hot oil until golden brown, about 30 seconds on each side. Drain on paper towels.

- Fill a large pastry bag fitted with a pointed tip with jam. Make a hole at the top of each doughnut using a toothpick or wooden skewer. Insert the pastry tip into the hole and squeeze about a tablespoon of filling in to each *sufganiyot*. Roll them around in some sugar and watch them disappear in seconds.

RICOTTA, PINE NUT,

A N D

HONEY BREAD PUDDING

Serves 6 to 8

WHEN IT'S NASTY OUTSIDE and you're in the mood for something sweet that doesn't require a trip to the grocery store, bread pudding will do the job. Though I love the taste of the ricotta and pine nuts here, this is a bread pudding recipe that can be layered with many other ingredients or even left alone with a drizzle of honey.

BOURBON CRÈME ANGLAISE

1 cup whole milk

1 cup heavy cream

3 tablespoons honey

3 large egg yolks

¼ cup sugar

Pinch of kosher salt

½ teaspoon vanilla extract

1 tablespoon bourbon

BREAD PUDDING

2 cups whole milk

2 cups heavy cream

¼ cup honey

3 large eggs

¼ cup sugar

12 cups cubed Challah (page 24)

1½ cups ricotta

¼ cup toasted pine nuts

4 tablespoons (½ stick) unsalted butter, melted

For the Crème Anglaise

- Combine the milk, cream, and honey in a medium saucepan. Heat the mixture over medium-low heat just until small bubbles begin to appear at the surface, about 5 minutes. Have a bowl of ice and water nearby.

- Whisk the egg yolks and sugar together in a mixing bowl, then very slowly add half of the hot milk mixture in a thin stream. Pour the mixture back into the saucepan and cook over medium heat, stirring frequently until the mixture is thick enough to coat the back of the spoon, about 7 minutes. Remove from the heat and strain into a bowl through a fine-mesh sieve. Stir in the salt, vanilla, and bourbon and place the bowl over the ice bath to cool completely.

For the Pudding

- Combine the milk, cream, and honey in a large bowl. Whisk together the eggs and sugar, then add to the milk mixture. Whisk well to combine and toss in the challah bread cubes. Cover with plastic wrap and allow to soak for 15 minutes.

- Preheat the oven to 350°F. Line the bottom of a deep 9-by-13-inch baking dish with parchment paper and set aside.

- Gently fold the ricotta and pine nuts into the bread mixture using your hands. Drizzle in the melted butter and fold in. Transfer the bread mixture to the lined baking dish and cover with aluminum foil. Bake for 40 minutes, then remove the foil and crank up the temperature to 425°F. Bake until the top is a deep golden brown, 15 to 20 minutes.

- To serve, cut into individual portions and top with the crème anglaise.

JUST
THE TWO
OF US

ROMANTIC
DISHES

For better or for worse, my experience with romance is eerily similar to how I cook:

A handful of this, a pinch of that,

a bit of sour and lots of sweet, intuition instead of any set game plan, and tons of faith that it'll all work out in the end. And somehow it has.

I MET MY HUSBAND, STEFAN, in August 2001, two weeks before I married another man.

It was at a party in the West Village. After the party broke up, Stef and I stood outside on the sidewalk and talked for an hour as I halfheartedly looked for a taxicab that, secretly, I hoped would never come. When a cab finally did arrive, I hugged Stefan good-bye and cried. Something inside me knew.

The guy I flew back to Israel to marry had been a colleague of mine at my first professional restaurant job. He was tall and blond and had an encyclopedic knowledge of food. We'd been together for more than three years when we decided to marry, but it lasted only three months once we did. I'd had my doubts from the beginning, but it turned out my doubts were nothing compared with his. So when I came home from work one night and found our apartment bare, I was shocked but not exactly surprised.

A year later, I returned to New York for a visit, having no idea that I would never leave. My brother, Elon, picked me up from the airport and drove me to his apartment. A few hours later, Stef came to visit. With Stefan, there were never any doubts. We quickly became a couple and moved in together within a month. A few weeks later he turned to me one morning in bed and said, "So? Are we getting married?" We took the N train to City Hall and were husband and wife by supper.

So, no, it wasn't the most wonderful thing in the world to be thirty-one years old and divorced. But if the ordeal had led me to Stefan, how could I complain? In Stef, I'd found my perfect complement—which is a nice way of saying that in many ways we're complete opposites, yet somehow we manage to bring out each other's best. We shine more brightly together than we ever would on our own. I'm loud, I speak my mind, I can't keep a secret—I am completely unrefined. Stef, meanwhile, is quiet and reserved. Thoughtful. I am a steaming hot bucket of chicken wings, dripping with sauce. Stefan is a perfectly cultured wine made from the finest grapes on the vine. Neither like the other and yet together a delight.

Not that our marriage is all milk and honey. Like any couple, we face the usual challenges, plus a not-so-typical one: we run our three restaurants together. As chef, I'm the face of Balaboosta and Taïm. I concoct the recipes and assemble the menu, and I get to accept any praise that comes our way. Everything else—from payroll to fixing a broken refrigerator to managing the waitstaff—is handled by Stef. It's a thankless job, one that's required him to put his own ego aside for the benefit of what we created together.

I've also come to rely on Stef as my test-palate-in-chief. Anytime I develop a new recipe, I let him try it first and anxiously await his endorsement before adding it to the menu. Obviously, this requires an enormous amount of trust. When he approves, I feel high. When he doesn't, it hurts. But he's always right.

Hollywood seems to think there's nothing more romantic than a bowl of fresh strawberries dipped in whipped cream. For me, though, what truly makes a food romantic isn't the texture or how it looks but what you, as a partner, can give. I'm never more flattered than when I wake up on a Sunday and find Stefan in the

kitchen, cooking a wild mushroom omelet with mushrooms he picked up at seven that morning. He could be toasting Wonder Bread for all I care. The fact that he woke up early and put in the effort to treat me right is what touches my heart.

Some of the recipes in this chapter might not be romantic in the way you'd expect. To be sure, a number of the foods have an element of sex: the whole artichoke with lemon aioli, for example, is fun to pick up and eat with your hands. Others are aphrodisiacs, like the sea scallops with citrus beurre blanc. One recipe—the beef tartare with harissa, which is a spicy, aggressive dish—appears to make no sense at all in a chapter dedicated to romance. But it's here because it's a perfect metaphor for the love between Stefan and me: intense, heavy, spicy, in need of careful handling, but full of aromas and layers of flavor that keep revealing themselves, the way Stef and I do to each other.

MORNING ORGASM COCKTAIL

Serves 2

WITH TWO KIDS WHO STILL like to finish the night in our bed, special morning time doesn't happen as often as I'd wish, so this drink has become a bit of a replacement. Pomegranate is a much-praised super food that's packed with nutrients and antioxidants. In other words, it's good for you! Great for a brunch cocktail.

2 sugar cubes
¼ teaspoon rose water
½ cup pomegranate juice
1 cup chilled champagne or sparkling wine
Two 1-inch strips lemon zest

- Place a sugar cube at the bottom of each of two champagne flutes. Divide the rose water, pomegranate juice, and champagne evenly between the glasses and garnish with a lemon twist.

COCONUT MILK FRENCH TOAST

Serves 2

FRENCH TOAST IS THE BEST solution for leftover or day-old challah. I use coconut milk in the egg mixture for a tropical flavor. I like to use this French toast to create the ultimate indulgent sandwich: two pieces of French toast with a healthy portion of cream cheese in between.

Cream cheese for spreading
Four 1½-inch-thick slices Challah (page 24)
5 eggs
1 cup heavy cream
⅓ cup coconut milk
2 tablespoons sugar
¼ teaspoon vanilla extract
1 tablespoon unsalted butter
Powdered sugar
Mixed berries
Maple syrup

- Preheat the oven to 375°F.

- Heat a large skillet over medium-low heat.

- While the skillet is heating, spread a layer of cream cheese on 2 slices of bread, then top each one with the other 2 pieces of challah to make a sandwich.

- Whisk together the eggs, cream, coconut milk, sugar, and vanilla in a large bowl. Transfer the mixture to a large baking dish and soak the sandwiches in the mixture for about 30 seconds on each side, allowing them to absorb the custard.

- Melt the butter in the hot skillet. Add the sandwiches and cook until golden brown on each side, about 2 minutes. Transfer to a baking sheet and cook in the oven for another 5 minutes.

- Cut the French toast on the diagonal to make four triangles. Place two pieces on each plate, dust lightly with powdered sugar, and top with a small handful of berries and some sweet, sticky maple syrup.

BEEF TARTARE

WITH

HARISSA

Serves 2

I GREW UP IN A KOSHER HOME, which meant that any time my mother prepared beef she first had to soak it in salt until every last drop of blood and juice was sucked dry. My mom would never even think to serve raw fish, let alone raw beef. No wonder I was never crazy about meat! Then I discovered all the better ways to prepare it. The harissa in this recipe is spicy, aromatic, and intense.

¾ teaspoon World's Best Harissa (page 272)

1 tablespoon finely chopped scallion, green part only

2 tablespoons finely chopped fresh cilantro

3 tablespoons finely chopped capers

Grated zest of 1 lime

2 teaspoons fresh lime juice

½ pound boneless beef sirloin, finely chopped

Pinch of kosher salt

1 tablespoon plus 1 teaspoon finely chopped toasted pistachios

2 slices baguette or sourdough bread, toasted

- Mix together the harissa, scallions, cilantro, capers, lime zest, and lime juice. Add the chopped sirloin and season with salt. Add the pistachios.

- Divide the tartare between the two slices of toast and serve.

WHOLE ARTICHOKE

WITH

LEMON AIOLI

Serves 2

AS A CHILD, I'D PULL A LEAF from the artichoke while it was cooking and taste it, only to have my mother scream, "Einat, *savlanoot*! Patience!" But pulling the leaves is the best way to know whether your artichoke is done; if they fall right off, you know they're ready. Artichokes go with all acids, which is what makes the lemon aioli such a nice dipping sauce. Try them with balsamic vinaigrette too.

1 large artichoke
1 bay leaf
3 garlic cloves
¼ cup kosher salt
1 lemon, halved
Lemon Aioli (page 268)

- Cut off the rough part of the artichoke stem and remove the tough outer leaves; discard.

- Place the artichoke in a large saucepan and cover with water. Add the bay leaf, garlic, salt, and lemon and bring to a boil. Lower the heat to simmer until the artichoke is nice and tender, about 45 minutes. Serve with lemon aioli.

RAW OYSTERS

WITH

WATERMELON GRANITA

Serves 2

IN HONOR OF MY TWENTY-seventh birthday, I threw a huge party on the roof of my apartment building in Tel Aviv. I treated my two hundred guests to a watermelon-vodka-lime Popsicle that was a huge hit. That combination of flavors is replicated here. I can't think of a better aphrodisiac than oysters, booze, and a summery fruit like watermelon.

WATERMELON GRANITA
1³⁄₄ cups pureed watermelon
1 tablespoon Simple Syrup (page 278)
Grated zest and juice of 1 lime
¹⁄₄ cup vodka

1 dozen oysters on the half shell

- Mix all the ingredients for the granita together. Place in an airtight container in the freezer for 1¹⁄₂ hours. Scrape the forming ice crystals with a fork and place back in the freezer. Repeat this process every hour until the desired crystals have formed.

- Place a dollop of granita over each oyster and serve immediately.

FRIED OLIVES

WITH

LABNE

Serves 2 to 4

THIS IS ONE OF MY SIGNATURE dishes that I just can't let go of—it's been with me from the time I created my first menu in New York. I serve it as an appetizer at Balaboosta, but it's also a great snack with cold beer.

Canola oil for deep frying
$\frac{1}{2}$ cup all-purpose flour
2 large eggs, beaten
3 cups fine panko
2 cups pitted Kalamata olives
Labne (page 271)
Harissa Oil (page 253)

- Heat enough oil in a skillet or medium pot to deep-fry the olives.

- Line up three large bowls on your counter and fill the first one with the flour, the second one with the eggs, and the third with the panko.

- Working in small batches (no more than 8 to 10 olives at a time) with the help of your trusty slotted spoon, throw a handful of olives into the flour and shake off any excess flour. Quickly dip the olives in the egg, then into the panko. Shake off the excess panko, then put the olives back into the egg mixture one last time. Transfer from the egg mixture back to the panko and shake them around to coat evenly. Shake off any excess crumbs with the slotted spoon and place in an airtight container until ready to use. This can be done up to a day in advance as long as it is stored in the refrigerator.

- When the oil reaches about 375°F, carefully place a handful of olives in the oil using the slotted spoon. Fry until golden brown, about 1 minute. Transfer the fried olives to paper towels to absorb any excess oil.

- To serve, dollop the labne evenly across the bottom of a shallow serving bowl. Add the piping-hot fried olives in the middle. Carefully pour the harissa oil around the circumference of the bowl.

LAMB CHOPS

WITH

PERSIAN LIME SAUCE

Serves 2

I'VE NEVER BEEN MUCH FOR manners, which is especially evident when I'm digging into my favorite meats at upscale restaurants: many a time I've embarrassed my companions by holding a bone of lamb (or veal or rib-eye) and slurping the delicious fat straight off the shank. The sauce here is made with Persian limes, which are available at specialty stores or online and have just the right amount of acid to cut through the fat of the lamb.

PERSIAN LIME SAUCE
1 tablespoon unsalted butter
1 medium shallot, coarsely chopped
3 garlic cloves, coarsely chopped
2 tablespoons sugar
2 tablespoons kosher salt
¼ teaspoon freshly ground black pepper
3 dried Persian limes, finely ground
4 cups chicken stock
¼ cup Greek yogurt, drained

LAMB CHOPS
6 to 8 rib lamb chops
Kosher salt
Freshly ground black pepper
Olive oil

For the Lime Sauce

- Melt the butter in a medium saucepan over medium-low heat, add the shallot, and sauté until soft, about 3 minutes. Add the garlic and sauté for another 2 minutes. Add the sugar, salt, pepper, limes, and chicken stock and bring to a boil. Lower the heat to simmer and reduce the liquid by half. Remove from the heat and allow the sauce to cool for 15 minutes. Puree in a food processor and blend with the yogurt. The sauce can be made up to 1 day in advance and reheated when ready to use.

For the Lamb Chops

- Place a large skillet over high heat for 5 to 7 minutes to get your pan nice and hot for that perfectly seared meat. Generously season the lamb chops with salt and pepper on both sides. Add a drizzle of olive oil to the skillet, then add the chops and sear for 3 minutes on one side. Flip the chops and sear for another 2 minutes for medium-rare.

- Place a spoonful of the Persian lime sauce onto individual plates and top with the lamb chops. Skip the utensils and use your fingers to hold the chops while you gnaw the meat off the bone.

ONE BIG STEAK

FOR

TWO

Serves 2, with 2 cups sauce

MEN LOVE SEX. AND STEAK.
So if you really want to impress your man, I can help you with the second one. The truth is, you don't need much skill or effort. Just pick up a good piece of meat—my favorite is a juicy marbled, aged ribeye. Then follow the recipe here and you've won him for life.

CHIMICHURRI SAUCE

½ cup fresh cilantro

Leaves from 1 fresh oregano sprig

1 bay leaf

1 large jalapeño chile, cored, seeded, and coarsely chopped

3 garlic cloves

¾ cup canola oil

2 tablespoons white wine vinegar

1½ teaspoons kosher salt

Pinch of freshly ground black pepper

½ cup fresh flat-leaf parsley leaves

STEAK

One 2-inch-thick bone-in ribeye steak

Kosher salt

Freshly ground black pepper

For the Chimichurri

- Combine all the ingredients except the parsley in a food processor until finely chopped. Add the parsley and pulse until a pestolike consistency is reached. The sauce is best served fresh, but it can be made up to 3 days in advance. If making ahead, transfer to an airtight container and refrigerate until ready to use.

For the Steak

- Preheat the oven to 450°F. Let the steak and chimichurri return to room temperature.

- Generously season one side of the steak with salt and pepper. Meanwhile, heat a large skillet, preferably cast iron, over medium heat. A really hot pan is the key to this great big steak, so leave the skillet on the stove for about 10 minutes.

- Now is the time to open up all your windows, because it's going to get smoky! Place the seasoned side of the steak down on the skillet and sear for 3 minutes. Season the top with salt and pepper, then flip it. Sear for another 2 minutes and place in the oven for 10 minutes for medium-rare. Allow the meat to rest on a cutting board for 5 minutes before cutting into it.

- Serve the steak with the chimichurri sauce in a small ramekin or add a dollop right on top.

CRISPY CALAMARI

WITH

SAFFRON AIOLI

Serves 2

CALAMARI IS ONE OF THOSE foods that's just so much better when it's fried. The flour mixture here is composed of rice flour, regular flour, and cornstarch, which keeps it crunchy. Tangy saffron aioli offers much needed lemon and acid.

Canola oil for deep frying
$\frac{1}{2}$ pound cleaned calamari, cut into rings
Kosher salt
Freshly ground black pepper
$\frac{1}{2}$ cup rice flour
$\frac{1}{4}$ cup all-purpose flour
2 teaspoons cornstarch
Saffron Aioli (page 269)

- Heat 3 inches of canola oil in a deep skillet until the temperature reaches 375°F.

- Pat the calamari dry with a few paper towels and season with salt and pepper.

- Combine the rice flour, all-purpose flour, and cornstarch in a medium bowl. Toss the calamari into the mixture and coat thoroughly. Dust off the excess flour and fry the calamari in small batches until golden brown, 2 to 3 minutes. Drain on paper towels and season with salt. Serve hot with a side of the aioli.

SEA SCALLOPS

WITH

CITRUS BEURRE BLANC

Serves 2

THIS IS A STRAIGHTFORWARD, easy-to-make recipe. When scallops are fresh, it's hard to mess them up; this recipe just aims to take advantage of what's already there. The citrus sauce is light and fresh, with a tad of bitterness and acid to cut the scallop's natural sweetness.

CITRUS BEURRE BLANC

¼ cup finely chopped shallots

¼ cup champagne vinegar

¼ cup fresh grapefruit juice

10 tablespoons unsalted butter, cut into small cubes

2½ teaspoons kosher salt

6 to 8 sea scallops

1 tablespoon unsalted butter

Sea salt

6 blood orange or grapefruit segments

- To make the citrus beurre blanc, combine the shallots, vinegar, and grapefruit juice in a small saucepan. Bring to a boil, then lower the heat to simmer and reduce by half, 6 to 7 minutes. Whisk in 5 tablespoons of the butter, then remove from the heat and add the remaining 5 tablespoons butter. Season with salt and keep warm.

- Remove the scallops from the refrigerator 20 minutes before cooking. Heat a large dry skillet over medium heat until it's hot, hot, hot, about 10 minutes. Meanwhile, gently dab the scallops with paper towels to remove any excess water. When the skillet is ready, melt the tablespoon of butter in it, add the scallops, and sear for 1 minute on each side. Remove from the pan and sprinkle a pinch of sea salt on each side.

- To serve, spread a spoonful of the beurre blanc at the bottom of the plate, place the scallops on top, and garnish with the blood orange segments.

CRISPY KALE

WITH

NIGELLA

AND

SESAME SEEDS

Serves 2

KIND OF LIKE THE WAY I FOUND Stefan, I didn't discover kale until much later in life, but when I did I immediately fell in love. These days you can find crispy kale at gourmet grocery stores. But this homemade snack tops all the others by far. And it can be made in 30 minutes from start to finish.

½ pound kale, washed and dried
2 teaspoons olive oil
½ teaspoon kosher salt
1 tablespoon tahini (optional)
1 tablespoon lemon juice (optional)
½ teaspoon minced garlic (optional)
1 tablespoon nigella seeds (see page 49)
1½ teaspoons sesame seeds

- Preheat the oven to 275°F.

- Trim the stems and the tough ribs from the kale, leaving only the leaves. Rip the leaves into large pieces. Put the kale in a large bowl and toss with the oil and salt and, if using, the tahini and lemon juice. If you've been married for ten years like me and fresh breath has become overrated, throw in the garlic too.

- Place the kale in a single layer on a large baking sheet and sprinkle the nigella and sesame seeds on top.

- Bake until the leaves are completely dehydrated and crispy, about 30 minutes. If you happen to have a convection oven, you can prevent the leaves from flying all over the place by placing a sheet of parchment paper over them and then a cooling rack right on top.

- Cool completely, then transfer to a serving bowl. Proceed with your romantic evening.

TRUFFLE THREESOME

Makes 7 to 10 truffles

THEY SAY GOOD THINGS COME in threes. Here are three different coatings for truffles—cocoa powder, toasted pistachios, and chile. They are just as good separately or together.

4 ounces dark chocolate chips

1 ounce milk chocolate chips

3 tablespoons mascarpone

2 tablespoons unsalted butter, at room temperature

1½ teaspoons dark rum

½ cup pistachios, finely chopped

½ cup unsweetened cocoa powder

2 teaspoons pure ground chile, such as Aleppo or Caspian, or chile flakes

- Fill a medium saucepan with water and bring to a low simmer. Meanwhile, put all the chocolate chips in a large bowl and place right over the simmering water. Melt the chocolate chips completely, then stir in the mascarpone. Remove the bowl from the heat and mix in the butter, then the rum. Cover with plastic wrap and refrigerate for 3 to 4 hours, until the chocolate is firm enough to mold but not too hard.

- Line up three bowls. Put pistachios in one, ¼ cup cocoa powder in another, and the remaining ¼ cup cocoa powder mixed with the ground chile in the last bowl.

- You can shape the truffles by using a melon baller, but don't be afraid to use your hands to assist in this process. Getting a little messy is part of the fun! Make the truffles about ½ inch in diameter.

- Roll the truffles around in the desired coating and keep in the refrigerator or a cool dry place until ready to eat.

THE
BACKYARD
BARBECUE

RECIPES
BEST
ENJOYED
OUTDOORS

Whenever I throw a party outside,

the laughter is louder, heartier.

MAYBE IT'S BECAUSE THERE ARE NO WALLS, so people feel less inhibited and more willing to share the stories of who they are. Or maybe it has something to do with clothing—try as you might, it's hard to be serious when you're wearing flip-flops and shorts. Or perhaps it's as basic as the weather—that under a cloudless sky in the summer air, we're all simply happier.

As it is for most Israelis, outdoor eating was a staple of my youth. Every Yom Ha'atzmaut (Independence Day) Israelis flood the country's beaches, parks, promenades, parking lots—in short, any swath of public land they can carve out for their children and portable grills (we Israelis are mostly apartment dwellers; we do not have backyards) and celebrate out in the sun.

I grew up with thirty first cousins, a few of whom are older than their uncles and aunts. These Independence Day barbecues in the park, and the space they afforded, were literally the only chance we had to get the entire extended family together. Even now, I can close my eyes and see a montage of these barbecues: the dads and grandfathers in sleeveless shirts, their thick, spatula-wielding arms raking through the charcoal as smoke billowed up into the trees; the women, overdressed in skirts and head scarves, huddled in clusters around a picnic table as they wrapped potatoes in foil and mixed spices into marinating pastes for the chickens and meats; and the kids, some old enough to shave and some still in diapers, screaming as we played soccer and tag, the boys chasing the girls, the brave ones swiping just-off-the-fire, searing-hot, foil-wrapped baked potatoes for the rest of us between rounds. It is because of these Yom Ha'atzmaut cookouts that I know my cousins' names at all.

Now that I live in Brooklyn, it takes more effort to orchestrate these kinds of outdoor events. But I'm determined, not just so my own kids will enjoy the same experiences I did, but—and maybe more important—because I'm convinced that barbecues are how we are supposed to eat. Think about it: for millions of years, our caveman ancestors gathered around fires and swapped stories as they tore

into bison with their bare hands. They ran around and got dirty and didn't worry about keeping things sterile. Something tells me that our collective memory still craves the outdoor-eating freedom that comes with ripping into a dead animal under a blanket of stars.

And, of course, there's the food itself. Just as certain conversations can happen only out of doors, so too there are certain foods that must be prepped, cooked, and eaten outside to be appreciated fully. For example, kabobs. You can cook kabobs in a conventional oven. But do that and you deprive yourself of the whole kabob-eating experience, from the juiciness of the meat to the aroma of the smoke to the sense of freedom that allows you to wipe your greasy chin on the sleeve of your shirt. Part of it is psychological, but there's also a technical reason for this enhanced experience: when you cook kabob on a grill—i.e., over an open flame—you can heat the outside to a crisp shell while maintaining the juice within, and all while the meat stews in its own smoke, saturating each morsel with an earthy outdoor taste you simply can't achieve in your kitchen.

This is why even if you're not an outdoors person—or *especially* if you're not an outdoors person—I encourage you to try the recipes in this chapter. To never cook outside is to deprive yourself of a whole spectrum of flavors, textures, and methods.

MINT GINGER MOJITOS

Serves 4 to 6

ONE OF MY FAVORITE DRINKS, the Mojito, was created in Cuba, far from where I grew up. But somehow, Mojitos still remind me of home—probably because in Israel the use of citrus and mint is ubiquitous. The beauty of this recipe is there's no muddling involved. I like to make my Mojitos on the stronger side because the ice will eventually water them down. You can make yours lighter, or intensify the ginger flavor, or make it sweeter. After all, you are the bartender. Just be sure to label the Mojito container at your outdoor party "alcoholic"—otherwise, kids might think it's just limeade and you'll end up with a backyard full of inebriated eight-year-olds. For the virgin version, otherwise known as ginger mint limeade, simply omit the rum.

8 cups store-bought limeade
2 cups light rum
⅓ cup **Ginger Juice (recipe follows)**
½ cup **Mint Syrup (page 278)**
Leaves from 1 bunch fresh mint
Ice
1 lime, sliced

- Combine the limeade, rum, ginger juice, and mint syrup in a large punch bowl, then give it a quick stir. Take the mint leaves and roll them around in your hands a few times to release their oils. Then simply drop them into the punch bowl and add some ice cubes and some of the lime slices.

- As you serve each guest from the punch bowl, garnish each glass with a lime slice and some mint.

GINGER JUICE

I usually make a lot of ginger juice at one time and then freeze it into little ice cubes so they're ready when I need them. It's a little more work, but it's worth it.

One 8-inch piece of ginger (or more, depending on how much juice is in it)
2 tablespoons water

- Peel the ginger and chop into fairly small chunks. Place it in a blender along with the water and puree. Strain it through a fine-mesh sieve. If it doesn't quite make ⅓ cup, add a little more water or puree more ginger.

Makes ⅓ cup

HARISSA

AND

HONEY
HOT
WINGS

Serves 4 to 6

WHO DOESN'T LIKE THE COM-bination of spicy and sweet? Be careful, though—harissa is oily, so if you don't watch out, your wings will go up in flames before they're cooked inside. It's a good idea to strain the harissa through cheesecloth ahead of time to extract some of the oil.

½ cup honey
⅓ cup olive oil
3 tablespoons World's Best Harissa (page 272)
2 tablespoons fresh lime juice
1 tablespoon kosher salt
3 pounds chicken wings, rinsed

- Whisk together all the ingredients except the chicken wings. Taste the marinade, and if you can handle a little more kick, add another dollop of harissa.

- Dry the chicken with paper towels, then coat thoroughly in the harissa and honey mixture. Allow the meat to marinate for at least 1 hour or up to overnight.

- Prepare a grill and cook the wings over a low flame for 15 to 20 minutes, flipping them over halfway through the cooking time. If you don't have access to a grill, bake the chicken wings in the oven at 375°F for 30 minutes.

HERBED MEAT KEBABS

Makes about 35 kebabs;
serves 6 to 8

I LOVE KEBABS—WHICH IS WHY
I can't help making them at any backyard party. These kebabs utilize the same combination of herbs that I add to many of my dishes: mint, parsley and cilantro. Here, the addition of grated onion keeps the meat moist. Even a well-fed sheikh would be proud of this dish!

You'll need about 35 skewers; if using wooden skewers, be sure to soak them for at least 1 hour in water first.

2 pounds ground beef
1 medium yellow onion, finely chopped
$\frac{1}{3}$ cup finely chopped fresh parsley
$\frac{1}{3}$ cup finely chopped fresh cilantro
1 tablespoon plus **1** teaspoon olive oil
1 tablespoon plus **1** teaspoon water
3 tablespoons finely chopped fresh mint
2 teaspoons kosher salt
1 teaspoon ground cumin
1 teaspoon sweet Hungarian paprika
$\frac{1}{2}$ teaspoon ground cinnamon
$\frac{1}{2}$ teaspoon freshly ground black pepper

- Put all the ingredients into a large bowl and mix really well with your hands. Shape the ground beef mixture into cylinders about 3 inches long and $\frac{1}{2}$ inch in diameter, put them on skewers, and keep refrigerated until ready to use.

- When the grill is fired up, place the meat kebabs over the heat and grill them until good and charred on each side, 4 to 6 minutes.

- Serve these kebabs hot off the grill with a side of Spicy Grilled Salsa (page 141) and Red Onion Parsley Salad (page 142).

SPICY GRILLED SALSA

Makes about 2½ cups

THIS DISH CAN BE MADE ONLY on the spot, so come prepared with your ingredients. What you're shooting for is salsa with a genuine smoky flavor. You can use it as a dip with tortilla chips or pita, but it's particularly good as a spread inside a kebab sandwich. At my backyard parties, this is served alongside the Herbed Meat Kebabs on page 138.

1 large red bell pepper
1 large green bell pepper
1 large red onion, halved
1 jalapeño chile
2 large tomatoes
3 cloves Roasted Garlic (page 273), finely chopped
2 tablespoons finely chopped fresh parsley
1 tablespoon olive oil
1 tablespoon fresh lemon juice
1½ teaspoons kosher salt
Pinch of freshly ground black pepper

- Ideally, you would roast your bell peppers, onion, jalapeño, and tomatoes over the grill, but using your broiler or an ungreased cast-iron skillet on the stove works just as well. In either case, get a deep brown, almost black, char on all sides of the vegetables, about 20 minutes. Remove from the heat and allow them to cool completely.

- Peel away all the charred skin from the bell peppers, jalapeño, and tomatoes. Remove the stem, core, and seeds from the bell peppers and jalapeño, then core the tomatoes. Chop everything up coarsely for a chunky salsa.

- Transfer to a serving dish and stir in the roasted garlic, parsley, olive oil, lemon juice, salt, and pepper.

RED ONION PARSLEY SALAD

Serves 4 to 6

I LEARNED THIS RECIPE FROM my close friend Nina. Like many of her dishes, it has a taste that reminds me of childhood. The tart and fresh taste of this salad is the perfect balance for the Herbed Meat Kebabs on page 138. The fresh onion goes so perfectly with the smoky taste of meat that you'll consider it essential to all of your backyard eating.

2 large bunches fresh parsley, stemmed and coarsely chopped

2 medium red onions, thinly sliced

3 tablespoons white vinegar

1 tablespoon canola oil

½ teaspoon sweet Hungarian paprika

½ teaspoon kosher salt

¼ teaspoon ground cumin

- Combine the parsley and red onion in a large bowl.

- In a separate container, quickly whisk together the vinegar, oil, paprika, salt, and cumin. Drizzle the dressing over the parsley mixture and toss together to combine.

ADOBO STEAK

Serves 4 to 6

THIS RECIPE CAME TO ME courtesy of a former boss at a Latin restaurant. I loved working for this chef, and he adored me—so on my last day at work, he led me into his office, closed the door, and asked me which recipe I'd like to take with me if I could choose only one. I didn't even have to think about it.

If you buy your steak the same day you're planning to grill it, feel free to skip the overnight marinade completely and just coat the meat with the adobo right before throwing it on the fire. The oil marinade works well to preserve the meat if you plan on cooking it within a few short days.

2 pounds skirt steak
½ cup canola oil
5 garlic cloves
1 fresh rosemary branch
3 tablespoons Mexiterranean Adobo (page 272)

- Marinate the steak in the oil, garlic, and rosemary overnight in the refrigerator.

- Prepare a grill. Wipe the excess oil from the meat and give it a good rubdown with the adobo seasoning. Place it directly on the grill over medium-high heat and cook to medium-rare, about 4 minutes on each side.

TANGY TABBOULEH

Serves 6 to 8

THIS IS SUCH A CLASSIC
Middle Eastern salad, yet most people never get the chance to try the real deal. What really differentiates my version is that I use a *lot* of herbs. Most tabboulehs have a greater portion of bulgur, but here the herbs take center stage.

1 cup medium bulgur
1 cup finely chopped fresh parsley
1 cup finely chopped fresh cilantro
4 scallions, finely chopped
¼ cup finely chopped fresh mint
1 cup diced tomatoes
Grated zest of 2 lemons
¼ cup fresh lemon juice
3 tablespoons olive oil
2 teaspoons kosher salt
Pinch of freshly ground black pepper

- Pour enough hot water over the bulgur just to cover it and soak for 10 minutes. The bulgur will absorb most of the water, and it should have a slight crunch when you bite into one of the grains.

- Meanwhile, toss together the remaining ingredients in a very large bowl. Add the bulgur and mix thoroughly. Allow the salad to soak in all the wonderful tangy flavors for 30 minutes before serving.

DORIT'S CABBAGE SALAD

Serves 4 to 6

MY BIG SISTER, DORIT—WHO is a terrific cook in her own right— came up with this recipe. How great is it to have chips in a salad! If you can't find Terra Stix at your local grocery store, use any root vegetable chips and crumble them.

⅓ cup white wine vinegar

3 tablespoons olive oil

3 tablespoons sugar

2 tablespoons soy sauce

8 cups thinly sliced cabbage

3 cups Terra Stix root vegetable chips

1 cup shredded carrots

½ cup toasted slivered almonds

¼ cup finely chopped scallions

¼ cup toasted sesame seeds

Raisins (optional)

- Whisk together the vinegar, oil, sugar, and soy sauce and set the dressing aside.

- In a large bowl, combine the cabbage, Terra Stix, carrots, almonds, scallions, and sesame seeds.

- Right before serving, toss the salad together with the dressing. You can throw in a handful of raisins if you'd like. Dorit never does, but don't worry—your secret is safe with me.

VEGGIE SKEWERS

Serves 4 to 6

BACKYARD PARTIES TEND TO be for meat lovers. But nowadays at least a few vegetarians are certain to be in attendance, and you want them to leave happy too. This recipe is my solution. Go ahead and get creative: you can try mushrooms, broccoli, kohlrabi—in other words, just about any vegetable you like that can be skewered. Sometimes I like to throw in some portobello mushrooms. They're so good even your carnivores will love them.

You'll need 10 wooden skewers, soaked in cold water for about 30 minutes to prevent burning.

1 large eggplant
1 large zucchini
1 large red bell pepper
1 large red onion
1 pint cherry tomatoes
¼ cup olive oil
1 garlic clove, finely chopped
1 teaspoon finely chopped fresh rosemary
1 teaspoon finely chopped fresh thyme
Kosher salt

- Soak the skewers in cold water for 30 minutes. Meanwhile, fire up the grill and get it nice and hot.

- Trim and slice the eggplant, zucchini, red bell pepper, and red onion and cut them into 1-inch chunks. Thread one piece of eggplant, zucchini, bell pepper, and onion and one cherry tomato on each skewer. Repeat the process until you've used up all your vegetables.

- In a small bowl, whisk together the olive oil, garlic, rosemary, and thyme. Brush each skewer generously with the marinade and season with salt.

- Place the skewers on the hot grill over medium-high heat and cook until the vegetables are tender, turning occasionally, 12 to 15 minutes.

ROASTED PEPPER TAHINI

Makes about 2 cups

YOU'VE ALL HEARD OF TAHINI—
it's a staple in the Middle East and now
a popular side dish the world over.
This version includes roasted red peppers, which add sweetness that reduces
the bitterness of tahini. A dash of sweet
paprika strengthens the color and
flavor.

2 large red bell peppers
1 cup tahini
1 garlic clove, finely chopped
¼ cup fresh lemon juice
½ cup water
2 teaspoons kosher salt
½ teaspoon sugar
1 teaspoon sweet Hungarian paprika

- Place the bell peppers directly on the hot grill or under a
broiler and roast until the skin is charred on all sides, about
20 minutes. Place in a bowl and cover tightly with plastic
wrap without letting the plastic wrap touch the hot bell peppers, or the plastic will melt. Let the peppers cool completely.

- Carefully remove the skin from the bell peppers, then cut off
the stems and scrape off the seeds. Slice the peppers into
large chunks and place in a food processor. Add the tahini,
garlic, lemon juice, water, salt, sugar, and paprika. Process
the mixture until smooth and creamy. Transfer to a serving
dish and serve at room temperature.

SPACE COOKIES

Makes about 24 cookies

FIRST, IT'S NOT WHAT YOU think. Second, it tastes even better than what you were thinking. Best yet, when you eat these space cookies you'll actually remember the experience ... and you can enjoy them without having to sit through Pink Floyd's *The Wall.* I make these cookies with tahini, giving them an earthy peanut butter taste. And don't worry—there aren't enough poppy seeds in here to make you fail your next drug test.

6 tablespoons (¾ stick) unsalted butter, cut into small cubes
⅓ cup sugar
1 tablespoon honey
1⅓ cups all-purpose flour
1 teaspoon baking powder
Pinch of kosher salt
½ cup tahini
2 tablespoons poppy seeds

- Preheat the oven to 350°F.

- Mix together the butter, sugar, and honey in a large bowl (using an electric mixer is easier on the biceps). Add the flour and baking powder, then the salt and tahini. Last but not least, fold in the poppy seeds.

- Drop teaspoonfuls of dough onto a parchment-lined baking sheet. Place in the oven until golden brown, 10 to 15 minutes.

TURKISH COFFEE BROWNIES

Makes about 16 pieces

TURKISH COFFEE IS UBIQUI-tous in Israel. This dessert has a caffeine kick that'll keep your party guests awake so they can enjoy every last bit of the delicious food you prepared. The cardamom gives these brownies an exotic taste that you likely haven't experienced in other desserts.

8 tablespoons (1 stick) unsalted butter, plus butter for the pan

⅔ cup all-purpose flour, plus flour for the pan

3 ounces 72% cacao chocolate

3 large eggs

¾ cup sugar

1¼ teaspoons ground espresso beans, or instant espresso powder

1 teaspoon ground cardamom

1 teaspoon vanilla extract

½ teaspoon kosher salt

- Preheat the oven to 325°F. Grease the sides and bottom of an 8-inch square baking pan with butter and coat lightly with flour.

- Melt the chocolate and the 8 tablespoons butter in a small bowl over a pot of barely simmering water. Meanwhile, whisk the eggs and sugar together in a large bowl until the mixture is fluffy and pale yellow. Whisk in the espresso, cardamom, vanilla, and salt until well combined.

- Remove the melted chocolate and butter from the heat and stir with a rubber spatula. Then very slowly add the chocolate to the egg mixture and mix until thoroughly combined. Sift the ⅔ cup flour into the batter and mix well.

- Pour the brownie batter into the greased pan and use a rubber spatula to scrape out all that chocolate goodness. This is the part where I usually lick the spatula if no one is looking. Bake the brownies in the oven for 25 to 30 minutes. You can check for doneness by sticking a toothpick right in the middle. If it comes out clean, you're only seconds away from chocolate heaven. Cool the brownies before cutting.

FAT LIKE ME

HEALTHIER OPTIONS

About a month ago I was rummaging through a shoe box of old photographs when my seven-year-old son, Liam, pulled out a picture and asked,

"Who's this pretty lady?"

I LOOKED AT THE PHOTO AND SMILED. Standing in front of Buckingham Palace was a svelte, suntanned twenty-one-year-old in oversized dark sunglasses. She was thin and beautiful.

"That's your mommy," I said with a laugh.

"But you're my mommy," Liam replied.

I stopped laughing.

I held up the photo and studied the young woman in the picture. Her perfect skin. Her lean, long limbs. The slight curve of her hips.

Where the hell did she go?

One of the best parts about being a chef is that I get to spend my day tasting as I create. As for the worst part about being a chef... well, take a look at the scale and you'll see what happens when you spend your day with food.

But the thing that really gets me is that I know plenty of women with absolutely perfect figures who find fault with their bodies. Even the *really* gorgeous ones would prefer a bit less of this, a tad more of that. So many women just can't be satisfied with how they look. I should know. I'm one of those women.

Of course, my body changed when I had children. Not that I've gone down without a fight. Anything but! Since Liam was born, I've tried every trick in the book to lose weight. I took pills—you know, the ones that are supposed to curb your appetite so you eat less? They worked like a charm, except that I'm a person who loves to eat. Then came the famous diets with the fancy names—Atkins, South Beach. The cabbage soup diet. The "master cleanse." For all I know, they would have worked great. But I missed the food.

When I realized I loved food too much to remove it from my diet, I decided to try exercise. I started with boxing at my local gym. Didn't work: each session made me feel starved, so I always rushed home to eat. (At least now if people make fun of my weight I can kick their ass.) I experimented with something called Zerona. (If you haven't heard of it, all I can say is it's kind of like being fondled by an octopus that shoots fat-melting lasers into your flab. Enough said.) When Zerona didn't work, I bought a fancy bicycle. Eight hundred bucks and used twice. If you want to see it, check out my ad on Craigslist.

Last and least, I purchased a European body shaper. It's pretty much like a treadmill, except instead of running you stand in one place while the base vibrates so fast that the fat supposedly jiggles right off you. Almost as much fun as being fondled by an octopus.

I'd love to say that there's a great lesson in all of this—that after years of dieting and exercise I've learned to embrace who I am, flabby tummy and all. That would be a lie. But here's a truth: I'm simply not ready to give up the foods I enjoy or the satisfaction I get from cooking—and eating—a perfect meal.

So while I haven't thrown away my body shaper just yet, I've decided that for the time being I'll go ahead and eat what I enjoy, but with one condition: that I eat as healthfully as I can. On most days.

And that's exactly what you'll find in the pages ahead: recipes for well-balanced, low-calorie meals that are as nutritious as they are delicious. Recipes like Marak Ktumim—literally, "Orange Soup," because everything that goes into it (butternut squash, pumpkin, carrots) is the color . . . well, you can figure it out. This vitamin-packed soup is one of my favorites these days, because it's zesty and tasty and has almost zero calories.

Exactly what a beautiful (or soon-to-be-beautiful) woman like me needs.

PEAR LEMON MINT SMOOTHIE

Serves 2 to 4

LOVELY IN ANY SEASON; PER-fect in summer. Choose your pears carefully so they're not too young or too ripe. This is already low in calories, but to make it even healthier you can substitute honey for the simple syrup. Be sure to drink your smoothie as soon as you make it—otherwise, it changes color from a beautiful light green to an icky gray-brown.

2 ripe Anjou pears

$\frac{1}{2}$ cup packed mint leaves

1$\frac{1}{2}$ tablespoons Mint Syrup (page **278**) or Simple Syrup (page **278**)

4 tablespoons fresh lemon juice

2 cups water

2$\frac{1}{2}$ cups ice cubes

- Peel, core, and coarsely chop the pears. Toss them into a blender with the mint, syrup, lemon juice, water, and ice cubes. Puree until smooth.

- I can't stress this enough, but be sure to drink this immediately before the pear oxidizes—trust me, that's not pretty.

GAZPACHO DUO:
MELON AND TOMATO STRAWBERRY

MELON GAZPACHO

Serves 4 to 6

MY CUSTOMERS AT BALA- boosta love my melon gazpacho (some even request it before they've seen the menu). The combination of flavors is a nice surprise—the melon, almond, and chile are beautiful together. At the restaurant I serve it with pieces of almond brittle broken up inside, but I left that part out because the brittle is sugar and we're trying to be healthy here... right?

1 ripe cantaloupe, peeled and seeded
½ **cup white wine (I like to use sauvignon blanc)**
¼ **cup sliced almonds**
1 fresh red chile, such as red jalapeño or a long red chile, cored, seeded, and coarsely chopped
2 teaspoons kosher salt
Pinch of freshly ground white pepper
Store-bought crispy fried shallots (see page 30) or onions
Chopped fresh mint
Finely chopped peeled jícama
Finely chopped fresh red chile (optional)

- Cut the cantaloupe into small pieces and place in a food processor. Add the wine, almonds, chile, salt, and pepper and puree until the mixture is smooth. Chill in the refrigerator before serving and garnish with the crispy shallots, mint, jícama, and red chile.

TOMATO STRAWBERRY GAZPACHO

Serves 4 to 6

THIS RECIPE WAS CREATED BY my friend Guy, whom I've known since we were in culinary school together in Israel and who today is the executive chef at Balaboosta. As with the melon gazpacho, we serve this in the summer. The strawberries add sweetness to the tomato's acidity without changing the color. This is also *very* simple to prepare.

5 large tomatoes, lightly scored

5 strawberries, plus strawberries for garnish

1 jalapeño chile, cored, seeded, and coarsely chopped

1 garlic clove, coarsely chopped

⅓ cup olive oil

¼ cup white balsamic vinegar

1½ teaspoons kosher salt

Pinch of freshly ground black pepper

3 cups ice cubes

Finely chopped red onion (optional)

Finely chopped cucumber (optional)

Croutons (optional)

- Bring a large pot of water to a boil, then carefully drop in the tomatoes. Boil just until the skin starts to crack and peel away, about 3 minutes. Remove the tomatoes from the pot and rinse under cold running water. When they are cool enough to handle, carefully peel away the skin and cut out the core. (If you want this gazpacho in a jiffy, skip this entire step and just go straight to the food processor, skin and all.) Slice the tomatoes into quarters and place them in the food processor.

- Add the strawberries, jalapeño, garlic, oil, vinegar, salt, and pepper. Puree the mixture until smooth. Next add the ice cubes and pulse until all the cubes are completely crushed. Garnish with sliced strawberries and any of the garnishes— red onion, cucumber, and/or croutons.

BUTTERNUT SQUASH

AND

SAFFRON SOUP

(MARAK KTUMIM)

Serves 8 to 10

BUTTERNUT SQUASH IS ONE of my favorite vegetables: it's sweet, tasty, and filling with barely any calories or fat. The soup is extremely rich despite containing not a drop of cream—kind of unbelievable, because the texture is so creamy. If you're trying to lose or maintain weight, this recipe is a keeper.

¼ cup olive oil
1 medium yellow onion, finely chopped
1 large leek, white part only, finely chopped
8 garlic cloves, finely chopped
5 pounds butternut squash, peeled and cut into ½-inch chunks
5 large carrots, peeled and cut into ¼-inch chunks
5 celery ribs, cut into ¼-inch pieces
¼ cup sugar
1 tablespoon kosher salt
2 teaspoons freshly ground white pepper
10 cups water
3 fresh thyme sprigs
1 fresh rosemary sprig
Pinch of saffron threads
Greek yogurt
Za'atar seasoning (see Note, page 77)

• Heat the oil in a large pot over medium-high heat. Add the onion and sauté until golden brown, about 7 minutes. Don't be afraid to let the edges turn a deep brown color, because this will give the soup an even better flavor. Add the leek and garlic and sauté for another 5 minutes. Add the butternut squash, carrots, and celery. Place a lid on the pot and allow the vegetables to cook for 20 minutes.

• Add the sugar, salt, pepper, water, thyme, rosemary, and saffron. Stir to combine all the seasonings and bring to a boil. Lower the heat and simmer until the vegetables are so soft you can press down on them with a spoon, about 30 minutes.

• Remove the pot from the heat and allow the soup to cool for 10 minutes. Puree the soup directly in the pot using an immersion blender. If you don't have one of these, allow your soup to cool completely, then puree in small batches in a blender.

• Taste and adjust the seasoning, then transfer the soup to another pot and reheat slowly before serving. Ladle the soup into individual serving bowls and add a dollop of Greek yogurt on top and a generous sprinkling of za'atar.

SALMON TARTARE

Serves 2 to 4

AS YOU'VE FIGURED OUT BY now, I'm mostly a Mediterranean cook. But I have a soft spot for the combination of avocado, tomatillo, and cilantro—a staple mixture of Mexican food. This recipe is one of my Cinco de Mayo favorites, and it's a cinch to prepare. I use Scottish salmon for this recipe, but king, sockeye, or even arctic char works beautifully.

3 medium tomatillos, husked and coarsely chopped
1 small jalapeño chile, cored, seeded, and coarsely chopped
1 cup packed fresh cilantro leaves
1 tablespoon white wine vinegar
¼ teaspoon kosher salt
One 8-ounce skinless Scottish salmon fillet
1 small fresh red chile, seeded and cut into very tiny cubes
½ small jícama, peeled and cut into small cubes (about ½ cup)
½ small avocado, cut into small cubes
1 tablespoon fresh lime juice
1 tablespoon finely chopped red onion
1 tablespoon finely chopped fresh cilantro

- Combine the tomatillos, jalapeño, cilantro, vinegar, and salt in a food processor. Pulse until all the ingredients are finely chopped and mixed thoroughly. Scrape the mixture into a plastic container and store in the refrigerator until ready to use.

- Cut the salmon fillet into ⅛-inch cubes and place them in a medium bowl. Add the red chile, jícama, avocado, lime juice, red onion, and finely chopped cilantro, then toss all the ingredients together. Pour the tomatillo sauce over the salmon and mix until well combined.

- Some people serve tartare with potato chips, but try to substitute the fried ones for the baked variety, to make this a healthier meal.

WHOLE ROASTED FISH

Serves 4

THIS IS THE CLASSIC MEDI-
terranean preparation for fish, without
all the fancy filleting, searing, steaming, or curing. The key is to layer the
ingredients inside the fish, instead of
on top, so that the flavor permeates
every last ounce of the meat.

Four 1¼-pound whole branzino, gutted and cleaned
4 fresh thyme sprigs
4 fresh rosemary sprigs
4 garlic cloves
1 lemon, sliced into 8 rounds
Olive oil

YOGURT DILL SAUCE
¾ cup nonfat yogurt
1 garlic clove, coarsely chopped
2 tablespoons fresh lemon juice
½ teaspoon kosher salt
1 tablespoon olive oil
1 tablespoon finely chopped fresh dill

- Preheat the oven to 350°F.

- Pat the skin dry on the branzino with a few paper towels.
  Stuff the cavity of each fish with one sprig each of thyme and
  rosemary, one garlic clove, and two slices of lemon. Place
  the fish on a baking sheet lined with parchment paper and
  drizzle with olive oil.

- Roast in the oven until cooked all the way through, about
  30 minutes.

- Meanwhile, make the yogurt dill sauce: Combine the yogurt,
  garlic, lemon juice, and salt in a blender. Puree until smooth,
  then very slowly add the olive oil in a thin stream. Scrape the
  yogurt mixture into a bowl and stir in the chopped dill. The
  sauce can be made ahead of time and kept in an airtight container in the refrigerator until ready to use.

- Serve each fish with the yogurt dill sauce and a side of the
  Beet and Walnut Salad on page 170 to complete this Mediterranean meal.

QUINOA SALAD

WITH

PRESERVED LEMON

AND

CHICKPEAS

Serves 4 as a main course,
8 as a side dish

QUINOA IS THE ROCK STAR OF grains, and with good reason: it's a complete protein, to the point where just 1/2 cup has almost the same protein value as a 12-ounce steak. Some complain that quinoa is bland and dry, so I've enhanced it with lemon, cilantro, chickpeas, and shallots for flavor and texture. Great as a side dish or a full meal.

Kosher salt

1 1/2 cups uncooked quinoa, rinsed

1/3 cup canned chickpeas, drained and rinsed

1/4 cup thinly sliced Perfect Preserved Lemons (page 276)

1/4 cup dried cranberries

1/4 cup finely chopped fresh cilantro

1/4 cup store-bought crispy shallots (see page 30) or onions

2 tablespoons fresh lemon juice

1 tablespoon olive oil

Pinch of freshly ground black pepper

- Bring a large pot of salted water to a boil, then add the quinoa. Cook for 12 minutes, then drain in a fine-mesh sieve and rinse under cold running water. Allow the quinoa to cool completely.

- When you're ready to serve the salad, combine all the ingredients, including 1 teaspoon salt, in a large bowl and toss to blend all the flavors.

- If you're not planning on serving the salad immediately, hold off on adding the crispy shallots until the last minute so they don't get soggy.

ARUGULA LOVER'S SALAD

Serves 2 to 4

I'M NOT A SALAD PERSON. BUT
if you force me to eat it, I'll insist on
arugula. Why? Arugula has spice and
character and is delicious with the
addition of just lemon and oil. But it
gets *really* good when you throw in
strawberries, almonds, and fennel—
sweet, tart, and crunchy.

VINAIGRETTE

5 medium strawberries, hulled and coarsely chopped

½ medium shallot, coarsely chopped

3 tablespoons white wine vinegar

1 teaspoon honey

½ teaspoon kosher salt

¼ cup canola oil

2 tablespoons olive oil

SALAD

6 to 8 fistfuls arugula (more if you really love arugula)

¼ cup toasted sliced almonds

½ medium fennel bulb, cored and thinly sliced

½ pint strawberries, thinly sliced

For the Vinaigrette

- Put the strawberries, shallot, vinegar, honey, and salt in a
food processor and pulse until the mixture is finely chopped.
Keep the machine running and slowly pour in the canola
and olive oils in a thin steady stream. Run it for a few more
seconds to mix thoroughly and add more salt if needed. You
can store the vinaigrette in an airtight container in the refrigerator for 3 to 5 days.

For the Salad

- Combine all the ingredients in a large bowl. Drizzle on just
enough vinaigrette to coat the salad lightly. If you get too
greedy with the dressing, your salad will turn out limp, and
nobody likes that. Toss everything together until well
combined.

BEET
AND
WALNUT
SALAD

Serves 2 to 4

THE GOOD NEWS: BEETS ARE jam-packed with nutrients. The weird news: a couple hours after eating this dish, you'll pee red. This can be alarming if you're not expecting it; more than one worried friend has called me, in confidence, only to have me reassure them that it's the beets, not their kidneys. To be completely honest, I'd prefer candied walnuts over plain roasted, but roasted are healthier. This makes a great lunch or side dish for grilled fish.

2 large beets

1 medium orange

$^3/_4$ cup coarsely chopped walnuts, toasted

3 tablespoons finely chopped fresh parsley

$^1/_4$ cup distilled white vinegar

3 tablespoons olive oil

1$^1/_2$ tablespoons honey

1 teaspoon ground cumin

1 teaspoon kosher salt

1 teaspoon freshly ground black pepper

- Place the beets in a large pot and add enough water to cover. Bring to a boil, then lower the heat and simmer until tender, about 45 minutes. Remove from the heat and cool the beets completely before handling. This step can usually be done up to 1 day in advance.

- When the beets are completely cooled, remove and discard the skin. Cut the beets into $^1/_4$-inch bits and place in a large bowl. Next, grate the zest of the entire orange over the beets and reserve the orange for a healthy snack another time. Add the walnuts and parsley and mix well.

- Whisk together the vinegar, oil, honey, cumin, salt, and pepper in a small bowl. Pour the dressing over the beets and toss everything together to combine.

OVEN-ROASTED BRUSSELS SPROUTS

Serves 2 to 4

USUALLY I FRY BRUSSELS sprouts. But a healthier option is to roast them, which gives them a candied taste. The sweet and savory flavors of this dish are so addicting, in fact, that you won't even realize it's good for you. To vary the flavor, try apples instead of pears and then add fruit or vegetable juice to impart moisture. This is one of the simplest recipes in the book—it takes a few minutes to prepare and another thirty to cook.

1 pound Brussels sprouts
¼ cup honey
1 garlic clove, finely chopped
1 Anjou pear, peeled, cored, and grated
2 tablespoons olive oil
¼ teaspoon kosher salt

- Preheat the oven to 400°F.

- Trim the bottoms from the Brussels sprouts and tear off the outer leaves. Cut the sprouts in half, then place them in a large bowl and add the honey, garlic, pear, oil, and salt. Toss together to coat the Brussels sprouts evenly with the honey mixture.

- Place on a baking sheet in a single layer and roast until tender on the inside and crisp on the outside, 35 to 40 minutes.

SWEET POTATO WEDGES

WITH

ROSEMARY

AND

MUSTARD SEEDS

Serves 4

SWEET POTATO WEDGES ARE the perfect side to steak, and they're a nice (and healthy!) change from the usual mashed potatoes or fries. The mustard seeds give these crunch, the honey a dab of sweetness. They almost taste like you're eating candy.

3 tablespoons olive oil
2 tablespoons honey
2 teaspoons mustard seeds
1½ teaspoons kosher salt
Pinch of freshly ground black pepper
1 fresh rosemary sprig
1½ pounds red-skinned sweet potatoes or yams, peeled

- Preheat the oven to 375°F.

- Whisk together the oil, honey, mustard seeds, salt, and pepper in a large bowl. Pick the leaves from the sprig of rosemary and add them to the honey mixture.

- Cut the sweet potatoes into 1-inch-thick wedges and toss them in the bowl. Mix well to coat the sweet potatoes evenly.

- Line a baking sheet with parchment paper and place the sweet potato wedges side by side in a single layer. Use a rubber spatula to scrape any remaining mixture from the bowl and drizzle it on top of the sweet potatoes.

- Bake the sweet potatoes until tender, about 1 hour, flipping them during the last 15 minutes of cooking.

PAVLOVA

WITH

BERRY COULIS

Serves 4

I'D LOVE TO TELL YOU I MAKE the best pavlova in New York, but I don't. For that you'll have to try the pavlova at Balthazar, where my husband, Stefan, used to work. I'd always been devoted to chocolate desserts, but when I tried the pavlova during one of the many times I was hanging out at Balthazar, I fell in love. My recipe adds a touch of vanilla. And I included it in this chapter because it's made of only egg whites, fruit, and a small amount of sugar, which you should feel free to vary.

Garnish this dessert with store-bought meringues, or just increase the recipe and make additional meringue, then shape into 3 mini-meringues per serving.

6 egg whites, at room temperature
1½ cups sugar
1½ tablespoons cornstarch
2 teaspoons white wine vinegar
½ teaspoon vanilla extract

BERRY COULIS
1 pint mixed berries
Grated zest of 1 lemon
1 tablespoon honey (optional)

- Preheat the oven to 275°F.

- Make sure your metal mixing bowl is clean of any oils or liquid and whip the egg whites with an electric mixer until soft peaks form. Slowly add the sugar 1 tablespoon at a time while the mixer is running. Adding too much at once will keep your egg whites from forming stiff peaks. Add the cornstarch, then the vinegar and vanilla. Whip until the egg whites are nice and glossy.

- Line a baking sheet with parchment paper and make 4 equal mounds of the egg white mixture directly on the parchment paper. Make a small crater at the top of each mound with a spoon—this will help hold some of the berry coulis later. Place the baking sheet in the oven, close the door, and immediately turn down the heat to 250°F. Putting the pavlova in a slightly hotter oven at the beginning will help it form a crispy outer layer. Bake for 45 minutes, until the pavlova has a nice marshmallow texture on the inside and a crispy crust on the outside. Resist all temptation to open the oven door and take a peek—this will cause the delicate dessert to collapse.

- While the pavlova is baking, make the berry coulis: Combine the mixed berries and lemon zest in a small saucepan and simmer over low heat, stirring occasionally to keep the bottom from burning. Cook until the berries are so soft they might just fall apart when you touch them, about 20 minutes. I like the coulis to be tart, but if you prefer it a little on the sweet side, add a tablespoon of honey. Cool to room temperature. Place a spoonful of the coulis right into the crater of the pavlova just before serving. Don't worry about the coulis overflowing—I think it looks more artistic this way.

WHEN DINNER CAN WAIT

SLOW-
COOKED
RECIPES

Most kids, at some point, have a goldfish.

Sometimes the goldfish is a planned purchase; sometimes it's won as a prize from the local county fair. I, too, had a fish when I was a child. Except instead of just one, it was a series of fish. And instead of goldfish, they were carp.

Y OU SEE, THREE OR FOUR TIMES A YEAR, when the big Jewish holidays rolled around, my mother went to Benny Ha-Dayag ("Benny the Fisherman"), the most famous fish market in Tel Aviv, where she'd purchase carp for that Friday night's Sabbath dinner. She'd visit Benny's on a Wednesday and would bring the carp, usually two or more, home in a cooler and set them free in our family bathtub.

Immediately, the carp became family pets. My sister, Dorit, and I would rush to the local pet store and buy fish food. My little brother, Elon, always wanted to name our fish, but Dorit and I forbade him: older and wiser, we knew their ultimate destiny, and we didn't want Elon to get too attached.

Keeping fish in the tub presented challenges. Beginning Wednesday afternoon, no one in the family was allowed to bathe. As the week continued, the tension mounted. Should we kill our fish early so that we could wash ourselves? Or keep them alive as we, ironically, began to smell worse than the fish?

Then there was the question of how to show off my new pets to my friends. I wanted so badly to invite classmates to the house so we could play with my fish and feed them together. But how could I explain that our fish were not kept in the tank, the way a normal family would, but in our *bathtub*? And how to convey the urgency of a visit—that anyone wanting to meet my pets had to do so now, *today,* because by next week it would be far too late?

Friday, around lunchtime, my mother transported the carp to the kitchen counter and smashed them on the head with a rolling pin. This, apparently, is the kindest way to kill a fish. I have no memories of the actual moment of impact—like any good *balaboosta,* my mother made sure I left the room for this violent act. But I do remember the sight of the kitchen afterward: scales smeared across the cabinets, bones and fish guts littered across the floor. Mine was a safe neighborhood, but if there ever were such a thing as *CSI Bnei Brak,* this is what it would have looked like.

After sundown, once my father had returned from synagogue, we'd gather around the table for dinner—chicken, potatoes, rice, and, of course, carp. No longer were our pets swishing their tails with joy, as they had just hours before in the tub. Instead, they lay motionless on a bed of carrots, onions, lemon wedges, and tomatoes, spiced with paprika, coriander, and turmeric. I tell this story not because I think you should raise appetizers in your bathroom, but to make a point: sometimes, if you want your meal to turn out right, it's worth the extra wait.

The recipes in the pages that follow have one ingredient in common: time. They don't all take a long time to prepare—Yemenite soup, for example, can be prepped in twenty minutes. But to get it just right, you need to simmer it for at least three hours— enough time for the spices, vegetables, meat, and marrow to meld together into a rich broth. Likewise with lamb—I cook mine for up to seven hours; I know it's ready when it softens off the bone.

An interesting side note: many slow-cooked recipes, including a few in this chapter, were discovered by accident. Observant Jews are forbidden to kindle a flame on the Sabbath, so the old *balaboostas* used to prepare all the food they'd need for the next twenty-four hours on Friday morning and then cook it over a low flame throughout the Sabbath. What they discovered is that everything tastes richer when it's cooked slowly. This is expected in soups and stews, of course, where the juices and spices have a chance to blend together. But it's also true for foods like rice, hard-boiled eggs, and even bread.

When you cook slowly, your foods end up looking different from what you're used to. At my falafel place, Taïm, we used to serve 5,000-Year-Old-Eggs (page 195) and people were surprised that the actual eggs, not just the shells, were brown—the result of stewing them overnight in a broth of onion peels and tea. So, yes, some of your foods may turn out looking strange. But trust me—it's not nearly as strange as eating your pet for dinner.

YEMENITE OXTAIL SOUP

Serves 4 to 6

AS THE DAUGHTER OF A Yemenite man, I ate this soup pretty much every Friday night of my child-hood. What really makes this soup unique is *hawaij*—a mixture of dried spices including coriander, turmeric, and black pepper that meld together with the meat and bones as the entire concoction slow-cooks for hours. If you're lucky, you can find *hawaij* ready-made at specialty gourmet stores. But there's no need: the recipe is here.

2½ pounds oxtails
2½ tablespoons canola oil
3 quarts cold water
1 medium yellow onion
1 head garlic, ends trimmed, unpeeled
1 celery rib, cut into 4 pieces
1 large carrot, cut into large chunks
1 medium tomato, grated (about ½ cup)
2 bay leaves
½ cup finely chopped fresh cilantro
½ pound butternut squash, cut into large chunks with skin on
2 tablespoons tomato paste
2 medium potatoes, peeled and cut into large chunks
3 tablespoons kosher salt
2 tablespoons Hawaij (recipe follows)

- Heat a large Dutch oven or other large, heavy pot over medium-high heat until it's hot, about 7 minutes. Meanwhile, rinse the oxtails and dry them thoroughly with some paper tow-els. Put the canola oil into your hot Dutch oven, add the oxtails, and sear until a brown crust appears on all sides. Carefully add the water and watch out, because the oil will splatter in the beginning. Bring this mixture to a boil, then skim off the yucky scum from the surface.

- Add the onion, garlic, celery, carrot, tomato, bay leaves, cilan-tro, butternut squash, and tomato paste to the pot. Bring back to a boil and add the potatoes, salt, and *hawaij*.

- Bring to a boil once more, then lower the heat to produce a really low simmer. Cover and cook for 3 hours.

HAWAIJ

I prefer to make my own *hawaij* because, let's face it, home-made is always better. You can even double the recipe and store the leftover mixture in the freezer.

1 tablespoon ground coriander
1 tablespoon ground cumin
2 teaspoons ground turmeric
2 teaspoons freshly ground black pepper
1 teaspoon ground cardamom

- Combine all the spices in a small bowel and mix thoroughly.

Makes ¾ cup

LAMB SHANKS

Serves 4

LAMB IS A TOUGH CUT OF meat, so preparing it well takes patience. You'll know your lamb is ready when the meat begins to separate from the bone slowly; only then should you check and see if it's soft enough to serve. Cooking the meat at a low temperature for a long time makes it wonderfully tender. If you don't have wine, braise it in broth. I recommend you get the smallest shanks possible so that each person gets one.

The recipe calls for 2 cups of wine. I usually gather up whatever wine we have left over from the previous night instead of opening up a new bottle. I've even been known to combine two or three different bottles, and yes, I even mix up the reds with whites.

4 lamb shanks, about 5 pounds
1½ tablespoons kosher salt
1½ teaspoons freshly ground black pepper
2 tablespoons canola oil
1 medium yellow onion, cut into large chunks
1 leek, white and light green parts only, cut into 2-inch strips
2 medium carrots, unpeeled, cut into large chunks
2 celery ribs, cut into 2-inch pieces
2 cinnamon sticks, each about 2 inches long
1 clove
1 star anise
1 small dried red chile
2 cups red wine
4 cups water
5 dried apricots, coarsely chopped
4 pitted prunes, coarsely chopped
¼ cup raisins
2 tablespoons World's Best Harissa (page 272; optional)

- Preheat the oven to 350°F.

- Heat a large Dutch oven or other large, heavy pot over medium heat. Season the lamb shanks with 1½ teaspoons of the salt and ½ teaspoon of the pepper. When the Dutch oven is hot (after about 6 minutes), add the oil and the lamb. Sear the lamb shanks, turning them to brown evenly, until a light brown crust forms on all sides, about 10 minutes total. Remove the Dutch oven from the heat.

- Add the onion, leek, carrots, celery, cinnamon, clove, star anise, chile, wine, water, the remaining 1 tablespoon salt, and the remaining 1 teaspoon pepper; mix thoroughly.

- Place the lid on the Dutch oven and cook slowly, slowly, slowly until the meat is about to fall off the bone, about 2½ to 3 hours. Remove from the oven and carefully scoop out each lamb shank, then keep them warm until ready to use.

- Place a sieve directly over a medium saucepan and strain the cooking juices into the pan. Use a rubber spatula to gently press down on the vegetables in the sieve to extract any remaining juices from them. Discard the bits and pieces left in the sieve.

- Add the apricots, prunes, and raisins to the saucepan and simmer until the sauce is thick enough to coat the back of a metal spoon, about 20 minutes. Stir in a heaping spoonful of harissa to add some kick if you'd like. Remove from the heat, ladle the sauce over each lamb shank, and serve immediately.

HAMIN

Serves 6 to 8

HAMIN IS A TRADITIONAL
peasant dish. Basically, instead of
throwing out the leftovers from the
past week, the Jewish *balaboostas* of
the world threw all the meat, bones,
and vegetables from that week's meals
into a pot and let them simmer overnight. There are different ways to
prepare *hamin*—European Ashkenazi
Jews add *kishke* (intestines), while
the Sephardic Jews of Moroccan,
Yemenite, Iraqi, and Iranian descent
add spices, beans, barley, and wheat.
There's plenty of room here for variety; try adding quince or dates instead
of prunes.

You'll need cheesecloth and kitchen
string.

BASIC HAMIN

1 cup dried chickpeas, soaked in cold water overnight

2$\frac{1}{2}$ teaspoons kosher salt

$\frac{1}{2}$ teaspoon freshly ground black pepper

1 cup dried pinto beans, soaked in cold water overnight

1$\frac{1}{2}$ cups barley

1 pound stewing beef

2 medium potatoes, peeled and cut into large chunks

10 prunes

6 dried apricots

6 large eggs

2 bay leaves

3 large garlic cloves

SAUCE

7 cups water

5 tablespoons kosher salt

1$\frac{1}{2}$ tablespoons sweet Hungarian paprika

1 tablespoon ground cumin

$\frac{1}{2}$ teaspoon chile flakes

$\frac{1}{4}$ teaspoon ground cinnamon

$\frac{1}{4}$ teaspoon freshly ground black pepper

- Cut three 9-inch squares of cheesecloth. You will use these to make little sachets of chickpeas, pinto beans, and barley.

- Place the chickpeas, $\frac{1}{2}$ teaspoon of the salt, and $\frac{1}{8}$ teaspoon of the pepper in the center of one cheesecloth square. Gather up all four corners to make a loose sachet and tie it up with kitchen string. Repeat this process with the pinto beans, $\frac{1}{2}$ teaspoon of the remaining salt, and $\frac{1}{8}$ teaspoon of the remaining pepper in another cheesecloth square. Repeat with the barley, $\frac{1}{2}$ teaspoon of the remaining salt, and $\frac{1}{8}$ teaspoon of the remaining pepper. Set these sachets aside.

- Season the beef with the remaining 1 teaspoon salt and the remaining $\frac{1}{8}$ teaspoon pepper. Place a single layer of meat at the bottom of a 6-quart Dutch oven or other large, heavy pot. Then scatter in half of the potato chunks, half of the prunes and apricots, and all three cheesecloth sachets. If there is any meat left over, add it to the top with the remaining prunes and apricots.

Continued

- Nestle the uncracked eggs into the top layer of all the goodies along with the bay leaves and garlic.

- Whisk all the sauce ingredients together and pour the sauce over the *hamin* goodies. Place the Dutch oven on the stove over medium-high heat and bring to a boil.

- Preheat the oven to 200°F.

- When the *hamin* and sauce come to a boil, remove from the heat. Place a lid on the Dutch oven and bake overnight for at least 8 and up to 12 hours.

- The *hamin* is ready when you wake up the next morning with the aromatic scent of beef in your house.

REALLY-NOT-SO-SHORT RIBS

Serves 4 to 6

THIS IS A PERFECT DISH FOR wintertime—it's heavy and stewy and will leave you feeling stuffed until April. Like lamb, short ribs are a tough cut of meat and require a long time to cook. The ingredients here are ones that are likely in your fridge and pantry already: aromatic vegetables, rosemary, thyme, and chicken stock. The exception is *baharat,* a spice mix you can make yourself or get at specialty stores.

3 tablespoons canola oil

1 large carrot, coarsely chopped

1 large yellow onion, coarsely chopped

3 celery ribs, cut into $\frac{1}{4}$-inch pieces

1 large leek, white and light green parts only, cut into $\frac{1}{4}$-inch pieces

5 garlic cloves

4 fresh thyme sprigs

1 fresh rosemary sprig

1 bay leaf

4 cups red wine

4 cups chicken stock

$\frac{1}{2}$ cup honey

3 tablespoons kosher salt

$1\frac{1}{2}$ teaspoons Baharat (see page **264**)

1 teaspoon sweet Hungarian paprika

1 teaspoon ground cumin

1 teaspoon freshly ground black pepper

5 pounds beef short ribs, rinsed

- Preheat the oven to 350°F.

- Heat the oil in a large Dutch oven or other large, heavy pot until it starts smoking. Add the carrot, onion, celery, leek, and garlic. Sauté until the vegetables start to caramelize, about 15 minutes. Add the thyme, rosemary, and bay leaf and sauté for another 5 minutes.

- Add the wine and bring to a boil, then reduce the mixture by half. Add the chicken stock, honey, salt, *baharat,* paprika, cumin, and pepper. Bring to a boil one last time, then lower the heat to simmer.

- The next part requires a little more movement, so use a pair of tongs for this one. Sandwich the short ribs between a layer of vegetables on the bottom and another layer of vegetables on top. Ladle some of the sauce over the short ribs, then cover with a lid. Bake in the oven until the meat is fork-tender, $2\frac{1}{2}$ to 3 hours. Serve with the sauce.

SPICY CHILI

Serves 4 to 6

SECRET NUMBER ONE: I LOVE
Wendy's chili. Secret number two: I worked at a Wendy's when I was fifteen. (The chain lasted for a year in Israel.) But I swear I didn't rip off its recipe. My version calls for harissa, which gives it heat, spice, and a Mediterranean twist. I use kidney beans, but you can experiment with different kinds. If you're short on time, open a can of beans and make this dish anyway. Just be sure to rinse the beans well—canned beans are loaded with nitrates to keep them preserved.

1 cup dried kidney beans, soaked in cold water overnight
1 pound ground beef
2 merguez sausages cut into bite-sized pieces
Kosher salt
Freshly ground black pepper
3 tablespoons olive oil
1½ cups finely chopped yellow onion
1 large red bell pepper, cored, seeded, and chopped
3 garlic cloves, finely chopped
2 tablespoons tomato paste
1 teaspoon sugar
3 medium tomatoes, finely chopped
3 tablespoons World's Best Harissa (page 272)
1 teaspoon ground cumin
¼ teaspoon chipotle powder
2 tablespoons finely chopped oregano
About 4 cups water

- Drain the beans and transfer to a medium pot filled with water. Bring to a boil and cook for 30 minutes. Remove from the heat, drain in a colander, and set aside.

- While the beans are cooking, sauté the ground beef and merguez in a hot pan. Did I say hot? I meant *hot*. Otherwise, you'll end up boiling your beef! Season the meat with a little salt and pepper, then drain off the excess liquid. Set the meat mixture aside.

- Heat the olive oil in a large pot over medium-high heat, add the onion and bell pepper, and sauté until caramelized, about 7 minutes. Add the garlic and cook just until golden, about 1 minute. Add the tomato paste (this tones down the acidity), stir, and then sprinkle the sugar over the mixture. Add the tomatoes and cook for another 5 minutes before adding the ground beef and merguez. Stir in the harissa, 2 tablespoons salt, the cumin, the chipotle, ¼ teaspoon black pepper, oregano, and the 4 cups water.

- Add the beans and bring the chili to a boil, then reduce the heat to very low, cover the pot, and simmer for 2½ to 3 hours, adding more water if it looks a little dry. Chili is even better the next day, but haven't we waited long enough?

STUFFED VEGETABLES

Serves 4 to 6

THIS RECIPE REQUIRES SOME
technique—hollowing out a vegetable
is tougher than it sounds. For example, with zucchini, you need a tiny
spoon or even an apple corer to clean
out the insides without puncturing
the skin. Once you scoop out the insides
of the vegetables, you don't need them
in the recipes. But don't throw them
away! Instead, freeze them in resealable plastic bags and use in a stew,
sauce, or sauté another time. You can
also stuff eggplant, bell peppers,
squash, onion—it's your kitchen and
you're the boss.

2 large tomatoes

2 medium zucchini

3 large potatoes, peeled and soaked in water to prevent
browning

½ pound ground beef

1 cup jasmine rice

1 medium yellow onion, grated (about 1 cup)

3 tablespoons finely chopped fresh parsley

2 tablespoons pine nuts

2 tablespoons canola oil

1 heaping tablespoon kosher salt

1 teaspoon ground cumin

1 teaspoon sweet Hungarian paprika

Pinch of ground cinnamon

Pinch of freshly ground black pepper

SAUCE

3 medium tomatoes, peeled, seeded, and pureed (about
3 cups)

3 tablespoons orange juice

3 tablespoons tomato paste

2 tablespoons fresh lemon juice

1½ tablespoons sugar

1 tablespoon kosher salt

1 teaspoon chile flakes

1 teaspoon sweet Hungarian paprika

1 bay leaf

4 fresh thyme sprigs

Pinch of freshly ground black pepper

- Trim the tops off the 2 large tomatoes and scoop out the
insides, leaving about ¼ inch of the tomato flesh intact.
Reserve 1 cup of the scooped-out tomato and its juices and
store the rest to use another time.

- Cut the zucchini in half crosswise. Trim off the ends just
enough so that each zucchini tube can stand up. Using a very
small spoon, perhaps with the aid of a paring knife, carefully
scoop out the insides from the cut ends. Sometimes I use an
apple corer, a melon baller, or a grapefruit spoon—think Mac-
Gyver. Store the zucchini bits and pieces for use another
time. Repeat this process with two potatoes. With the remaining potato, slice ¼-inch rounds and set aside.

Continued

- Preheat the oven to 250°F.

- Combine the ground beef, rice, onion, parsley, pine nuts, oil, salt, cumin, paprika, cinnamon, pepper, and the reserved 1 cup of tomatoes in a large bowl and mix thoroughly.

- Start stuffing the tomatoes, zucchini, and potatoes with the meat mixture. Make sure you don't overstuff the vegetables, because the rice will expand when it cooks. Next take the slices of potato and line the bottom of a pan that is just large enough to hold the stuffed vegetables. You want them to fit snugly so that the vegetables create some steam, kind of like the inside of a subway in Manhattan during rush hour.

- Place the stuffed vegetables on top of the sliced potatoes and set aside.

- In another bowl, stir together all the ingredients for the sauce. Taste and adjust the seasonings if you wish. Pour the sauce over the stuffed vegetables, then cover the pan with aluminum foil. Bake in the oven for $3\frac{1}{2}$ hours, then serve immediately.

OVERNIGHT TURNIPS

Makes as many turnips
as you wish

MY MOTHER USED TO COOK
these overnight for the Sabbath and
holidays, splitting them in half on Saturday morning and then sprinkling them
with brown sugar and eating them with
a spoon as one might eat a grapefruit.
Otherwise, make them as a side dish.

Turnips, rinsed
Water
Brown sugar

- Preheat the oven to 200°F.

- Place the turnips in a Dutch oven or other large, heavy pot in a single layer and fill with just enough water to come up halfway. Cover the pot and leave it in the oven overnight or for at least 8 hours.

- Remove the turnips from the heat and cut them in half. Sprinkle with a little bit of brown sugar.

HILBE

Makes about 2½ cups

THE MAJOR INGREDIENT IN this sauce is fenugreek seeds. Alone, these seeds are terribly bitter, so to take it down a notch you need to soak them for at least 8 hours. (You can do this overnight, but that may not be practical since you need to change the water frequently.) The gel-like paste goes beautifully with *kubaneh* and in Yemenite soup. *Hilbe* is an acquired taste, made for the adventurous. The reward is that it's extremely healthy: it will actually lower your blood sugar and cholesterol.

½ cup fenugreek seeds
¾ pound tomatoes, coarsely chopped
3 tablespoons fresh lemon juice
½ cup cold water
2 tablespoons kosher salt
1 cardamom pod
1½ cups packed fresh cilantro leaves
2 tablespoons S'chug (page 275)

- Soak the fenugreek in cold water for 8 to 10 hours, changing the water frequently to rinse away the bitterness. Transfer the fenugreek to a sieve and drain completely. Or you can reserve the water and drink it to lower your cholesterol. It may be bitter, but you'll live longer.

- Combine the fenugreek, tomatoes, lemon juice, and water in a blender. Remove the cardamom seeds from the pod and throw them into the blender too. Puree the mixture until smooth, then gradually add the cilantro and the *s'chug*.

5,000-YEAR-OLD EGGS

Makes 8 eggs

BASICALLY, THESE ARE HARD- boiled eggs that have been slow-cooked overnight. You don't have to use tea leaves, but they add a distinct color and taste to the egg that's worth having. I suggest that halfway through the cooking process you slightly crack the eggshells. This allows the tea to seep in just enough to color the eggs and paint a jagged, lightning-like line along the eggs—a nice aesthetic touch that will impress your guests.

8 large eggs
1 tea bag black tea (Earl Grey works well for me)

- Preheat the oven to 200°F.

- Place the eggs and tea bag in a medium ovenproof pan. Fill with just enough water to cover the eggs and place a lid or a sheet of aluminum foil over the pan. Bake in the oven overnight, 8 to 10 hours.

- Multitask these eggs with the *kubaneh* (page 197) in the same oven and, to complete the Yemenite trifecta, a side of *hilbe* (preceding recipe).

OSOVO

Serves 4 to 6

THIS RECIPE, WHICH ORIGI-
nated in Uzbekistan, is a combination
of a few versions I've learned over the
years. Basically, it's overnight rice
with layers of flavor. It's super-simple
to make, and the result is amazing.
Feel free to play around with different kinds of meat and dried fruit.

3 tablespoons canola oil

2 large yellow onions, thinly sliced

¾ pound beef short ribs

½ pound stewing beef

3 tablespoons kosher salt

2 cups jasmine rice

10 pitted prunes, thinly sliced

5 dried apricots, thinly sliced

⅓ cup raisins

3 cups water

2 bay leaves

1½ teaspoons ground cumin

1½ teaspoons sweet Hungarian paprika

½ teaspoon ground turmeric

- Preheat the oven to 190°F.

- Heat a large Dutch oven or other large, heavy pot over medium-high heat. When the Dutch oven is hot, add the oil and sauté the onions until golden brown, about 10 minutes.

- Season the short ribs and stewing beef with 1 tablespoon of the salt. Add the meats to the pot and fry them up until nice and brown. Next throw in the rice, prunes, dried apricots, and raisins. Carefully pour in the water and stir in the remaining 2 tablespoons of salt, the bay leaves, cumin, paprika, and turmeric. Bring to a boil, then lower the heat to simmer.

- Place the lid on the Dutch oven and transfer from the stove to the preheated oven. Cook the *osovo* overnight or for 9 to 11 hours and the delicious smell will lure you from your bed into the kitchen.

KUBANEH

Serves 4 to 6

ITALIAN MOTHERS SLOW-COOK marinara sauce, and anyone with an oven can slow-cook a stew. But did you know there was such a thing as slow-cooked bread? *Kubaneh* is best made in a special aluminum pot that you can find anywhere in Israel but possibly nowhere else—it's round with an air-tight lid. If you can't get your hands on one, use a Dutch oven. A bit of history: since Yemenite Jews were very poor when they arrived in Israel, many of their recipes revolved around nothing but dough. *Kubaneh* is heavy and greasy, but it's worth the calories in my opinion, so be sure to try it at least once. It goes perfectly with Hilbe (page 195) and 5,000-Year-Old Eggs (page 195).

4 cups all-purpose flour, plus flour for the work surface
¼ cup plus 1 teaspoon light brown sugar
2 tablespoons kosher salt
1½ tablespoons plus 1 teaspoon active dry yeast
2 cups warm water
Canola oil for the bowl
2 tablespoons unsalted butter, cut into small cubes, plus butter for the pan
2 teaspoons nigella seeds (see page 49)

- Mix together the flour, ¼ cup of the brown sugar, and the salt in a large bowl. Create a well in the center of the bowl and add the yeast, remaining 1 teaspoon brown sugar, and ½ cup of the warm water. Let it stand until nice and foamy, about 5 minutes.

- Gradually mix in the remaining 1½ cups warm water. Dump the sticky mess onto a floured surface and knead the dough until smooth and elastic. Shape the dough into a large ball and place in a bowl slicked with canola oil. Cover with a damp cloth and place in a warm place. Let rise until the dough has doubled in size, 45 to 60 minutes.

- Meanwhile, grease the inside of a 3-quart Dutch oven with butter and don't be shy! Sprinkle 1 teaspoon of the nigella seeds on the bottom of the pan. When the dough is ready, divide it into five equal parts and shape into round balls. Place one ball in the center of the pot and the rest all around like petals on a flower. Cover with a damp cloth and let it rise once more for 20 to 30 minutes.

- Preheat the oven to 220°F.

- Place the cubes of butter all over the top of the dough and sprinkle the remaining nigella seeds on top. Cover tightly with a lid and cook overnight, 9 to 10 hours.

MALABI

WITH

ORANGE BRANDY SAUCE

Serves 4

MALABI IS A TRADITIONAL MILK custard. My version calls for the use of a mixture of heavy cream and milk instead of all milk. This is an easy recipe, but it absolutely must sit overnight. These days, most custard recipes call for gelatin, but I use the original cornstarch to avoid the glazed look. I prefer the texture this way too, but it won't necessarily hold up on its own—so serve it in a glass or a cup, not on a plate.

MALABI
1½ cups whole milk
½ cup heavy cream
⅓ cup sugar
¼ cup cornstarch
2 tablespoons water
1½ teaspoons rose water

ORANGE BRANDY SAUCE
1 cup orange marmalade
½ cup water
1 tablespoon brandy

Peanuts or pistachios (optional)
Sweetened coconut flakes (optional)

For the Malabi

- Combine the milk, cream, and sugar in a large pot over medium heat. Once the mixture comes to a boil, remove from the heat. While you're waiting for your milk not to boil over, dissolve the cornstarch in the water. When the milk comes to a boil, quickly whisk in the cornstarch along with the rose water and immediately remove from the heat.

- Pour the *malabi* into four individual serving cups or ramekins and refrigerate for at least 6 hours.

For the Sauce

- Mix together the marmalade and water in a small saucepan. Bring to a boil, then lower the heat to simmer and reduce to a little more than half, 20 to 25 minutes, stirring often to prevent the bottom from burning and the mixture from boiling over. If the foam looks like it's about to flow over, simply remove the saucepan from the heat for a few seconds and give it a quick stir before placing it back over the heat.

- When the mixture has a thick, syruplike consistency, stir in the brandy and cook for another 5 minutes.

- Remove the sauce from the heat and let cool in the refrigerator until ready to use. Just put it back on the stove over low heat and your sauce will melt right back to an ooey-gooey consistency.

To Serve

- Serve the *malabi* straight from the cups with a generous drizzle of the orange marmalade sauce and throw in a handful of chopped peanuts or pistachios and coconut flakes if you wish.

THINKING
ABOUT
HOME

MOSTLY
ISRAELI
RECIPES

Every town in America has one—

a restaurant featuring "home cooking" or "Mom's apple pie" or "fried chicken just like Mama used to make."

YOU SEE IT IN ISRAEL TOO— restaurants with a handwritten sign in the window advertising *ochel bayit*—literally, "food of home." The difference is that in Israel it isn't just the food that reminds you of home but the whole environment: the dishes are chipped, the silverware doesn't match, and the guy who takes your order is also the cook, busboy, and cashier.

It's kind of strange when you think about it. I mean, is there any other product that prides itself on reminding you of home? We hire plumbers because they can unclog a drain *better* than our husbands and dads. And I don't know about you, but if I came across a psychiatrist who promised to "listen just like Mom!" I'd turn the other way. And run.

Yet when it comes to food, home is exactly what we seek. I'm sure psychologists have their own theories, but if you ask me, I think we eat not just to nourish our bodies but to nourish our souls. Or, to get even more specific, we eat to be reminded of the people we love. That's why "Mom's apple pie" is more appealing than pie without the mom—the phrase evokes not just the thought of apples and cinnamon and dough but also of a woman in an apron, her flour-dusted forearms wrapped around you in a hug.

I say this not just as a scholar of food but also as someone who's relied on food for comfort when far from home many times in her life. The first time was when I was twenty years old. It was the week of my birthday. On my back was a rucksack stuffed with a sleeping bag, blue jeans, and enough T-shirts, socks, and underwear to last me a week. In my hand was a cardboard sign that read DEUTSCHLAND.

You see, in Israel it's tradition to take a postmilitary trip to some far corner of the world to celebrate your newfound freedom. Most Israelis head to South America or the Far East. But I didn't have the money for such a big trip. So when I saw a newspaper ad seeking young Israelis to work at pushcarts in German shopping malls, I opted for Europe, which I was sure would be cheaper to get to, instead. (You know those kiosks you see at the mall where foreign-born salespeople in their twenties sell everything from skin cream and monogrammed socks to sunglasses and mouse pads with your kid's picture on it? I wanted to be one of those salespeople.)

Problem was, the airfare to Berlin was as expensive as a flight to Bangkok. So I booked a ticket to Zurich and decided to hitchhike the rest of the way. I passed through customs at Zurich Airport and headed outside to the curb. It was ten in the morning and freezing. A few feet away, a pair of newlyweds (at least they looked newly married) kissed and then loaded a suitcase into their trunk. "I'm go Germany," I said to them in the best English I could muster. "You go north?"

And that's how I spent the next sixteen hours, hitching from the airport to Zurich city center, and then to the highway, to a roundabout, to an exit, and then exits to restaurants and gas stations and open fields beside the road. The upshot is that I met some truly unforgettable characters. (The German truckie who looked exactly like a German truck driver should—dark mustache, flannel shirt, thick-soled boots—and didn't speak a word of English but talked my ear off anyway comes to mind.)

But there was also a downside:

Rain.

Somehow, I picked the rainiest day in Switzerland's seven-hundred-year history to hitch cross-country. Once in a lucky moment I made it to a truck stop. But mostly I did my hitchhiking along the highway in the rain, my rucksack getting heavier on my back, and, in my hands, my DEUTSCHLAND sign growing ever more soggy.

As the rain pounded my face, I fantasized about being home. Not that I wanted to quit my adventure and return to Israel . . . But, oh! To be back at my dining room table! In dry clothes! And with a steaming-hot bowl of chicken soup, a dish of *s'chug,* and warm challah straight out of the oven! This, more than the comfort of my own bed, is what home meant to me: the tastes and smells of my childhood kitchen.

Ochel bayit—the tastes of home.

This chapter is filled with my favorite home-style recipes. Perfect for those moments when you long for the people you love.

RICE
FIT
FOR A
KING

Serves 4 to 6

MY MOTHER CLAIMS THERE are 356 recipes for rice in Iran—one for every day of the year. (Apparently there are nine fewer days in the Persian calendar. Different story.) This recipe is the one used to commemorate holidays. The potatoes are baked right in, and the rice is flavored with cumin seeds, carrots, and currants. I'm not sure how it got the name *orez ha-malachim*—rice fit for a king—but it is.

Kosher salt
4 cups jasmine rice
1 large potato, peeled
¼ cup plus 2 tablespoons canola oil
1 teaspoon ground turmeric (optional)
2 medium carrots, finely chopped
1 cup dried currants or raisins
1 tablespoon cumin seeds

- Bring 4 quarts of water and ¼ cup salt to a boil (it may seem like a lot of salt, but the goal is to cook the rice as you would pasta). Meanwhile, rinse the rice in cold water; repeat until the water is clear. Add the rice to the boiling pot and cook until it is almost tender but still crunchy in the middle, 5 to 7 minutes.

- Since you're cooking the rice for only about 10 minutes, there will still be plenty of liquid remaining. When the rice is al dente, drain in a fine-mesh sieve and rinse under cold water. Drain completely, then dump it into a large bowl.

- While the rice is cooking, slice the potato into ¼-inch-thick rounds. Heat ¼ cup of the oil in a Dutch oven or other large, heavy pot over medium heat. Stir in the turmeric. Arrange the potatoes in a single layer at the bottom of the pot, making sure that all the pieces fit snugly. Sprinkle a pinch or two of salt over the potatoes. Sauté them until crisp and golden, about 5 minues, then flip them over to cook the other side, about 20 minutes altogether. Remove from the heat.

- Heat the remaining 2 tablespoons oil in a skillet and add the carrots, currants, and cumin seeds. Stir frequently and sauté until the carrots are slightly softened, about 5 minutes. Remove from the heat and scrape the carrot mixture into the bowl of rice and toss to combine. Transfer the rice mixture to the Dutch oven on top of the potatoes, then drape a kitchen towel over the pot to prevent any steam from escaping. Place the lid right over the towel, gather the ends of the towel, and bunch them on top of the lid.

- Place the pot over low, low heat and cook until the rice is tender, about 1 hour. You can serve this dish two ways—by inverting the entire pot of rice over onto a large platter or by scooping the rice onto a dish and then placing the potato slices on top. I always hold my breath when I flip the entire pot of rice over, and it doesn't always have a fairy-tale ending. So I usually cheat and go the other route.

KIBBEH SOUP

Serves 4 to 6

PART OF ME WANTS ME TO call it Iraqi borscht, but that wouldn't do it justice, and I'm afraid the name would create too many misconceptions. This soup is tangy, thanks to beets and lemon being boiled together into a broth. My recipe uses a combination of rice flour and semolina instead of plain semolina, which is harder to find in the United States. I worry that this recipe won't be around in two generations—I don't know anyone except my sister, me, and a handful of Iraqi grandmothers who still make it. I'm relying on you to carry on the tradition!

SOUP BASE

- 3 tablespoons olive oil
- 1 tablespoon canola oil
- 1 medium yellow onion, finely chopped
- 1 medium leek, white and light green parts only, sliced into $\frac{1}{2}$-inch pieces
- 2 celery ribs, cut into 1-inch pieces
- 2 medium beets, peeled and cut into $\frac{3}{4}$-inch chunks
- $\frac{1}{4}$ cup kosher salt
- 1 tablespoon ground cumin
- $\frac{1}{2}$ teaspoon freshly ground black pepper
- 12 cups cold water
- $\frac{1}{4}$ cup fresh lemon juice
- $\frac{1}{4}$ cup sugar

KIBBEH

- 1 pound ground beef
- 1 medium yellow onion, finely chopped
- 1 celery rib, finely chopped
- $\frac{1}{4}$ cup finely chopped fresh mint
- $\frac{1}{4}$ cup finely chopped fresh parsley
- 2 tablespoons canola oil
- 2 tablespoons kosher salt
- $\frac{1}{2}$ teaspoon ground cumin
- Pinch of ground cinnamon
- Pinch of freshly ground black pepper
- 1 cup semolina flour
- 1 cup jasmine rice, finely ground
- 1 cup water

For the Soup Base

- Heat the olive and canola oils in a large pot, add the onion, and sauté until golden brown, about 15 minutes. Add the leek and celery and cook until soft, about 7 minutes. Add the beets, salt, cumin, and pepper. Cook for another 3 minutes, then add the cold water and lemon juice. Stir in the sugar until thoroughly mixed and bring to a boil. Lower the heat and simmer for 45 minutes.

For the Kibbeh

- Mix together the ground beef, onion, celery, mint, and parsley in a large bowl. Add 1 tablespoon of the canola oil, 1 tablespoon of the salt, the cumin, the cinnamon, and the

pepper. Combine all the ingredients thoroughly, then cover the bowl with plastic wrap and refrigerate.

- Next combine the semolina flour, ground rice, remaining 1 tablespoon oil, remaining 1 tablespoon salt, and water in another bowl. Mix thoroughly and let it stand for 5 minutes.

- To assemble the kibbeh, moisten your hands with a little water, then place a heaping spoonful of the semolina mixture in the palm of your hand. Shape it into a flat disk, then drop a full tablespoonful of meat into the middle. Carefully wrap the semolina flour around the meat mixture—it should be about the size of a golf ball.

To Finish

- Gently place the kibbeh in the simmering soup and cook for another 20 minutes.

MAMA CAROLINE'S PISTOU SOUP

Serves 4 to 6

MOST PEOPLE HAVE TROUBLE with their mothers-in-law, but in Stef's mom I got lucky: not only do we click, but she's a pretty good cook too. Stefan's mother lives in a tiny village in Provence. About once a week she goes to her nearby farmers' market to stock up on ten or more different kinds of beans, then comes home, shells them, and boils the beans together into a soup of vegetables and chicken or pork. I make mine without meat, so it's especially clean and fresh—it'll make you feel healthy just eating it. I suspect this recipe originated not in France, but in nearby Italy—note the pesto.

$\frac{1}{2}$ butternut squash, peeled, seeded, and cut into small chunks

2 medium potatoes, peeled and cut into small chunks

1$\frac{1}{2}$ cups dried pinto beans, soaked in cold water overnight

2 large carrots, cut into small chunks

2 medium leeks, white and light green parts only, sliced into $\frac{1}{2}$-inch pieces

2 celery ribs, cut into $\frac{1}{2}$-inch pieces

1 large zucchini, cut into small chunks

1 medium yellow onion, finely chopped

$\frac{1}{4}$ pound broad beans, shelled

$\frac{1}{4}$ pound cranberry beans, shelled

3 tablespoons kosher salt

1 teaspoon freshly ground black pepper

PESTO

$\frac{1}{4}$ cup grated Parmesan

1 garlic clove, coarsely chopped

3 tablespoons toasted pine nuts

2 teaspoons kosher salt

Pinch of freshly ground black pepper

$\frac{1}{2}$ cup olive oil

Leaves from I large bunch fresh basil

- Combine the butternut squash, potatoes, and pinto beans in a large pot and fill it three-quarters full with water. Cover with a lid, bring to a boil, and boil for 15 minutes.

- Add all the remaining vegetables, beans, salt, and pepper. Place the lid back on, bring to a boil again, then lower the heat and simmer for 30 minutes.

- Meanwhile, make the pesto: Combine the cheese, garlic, pine nuts, salt, and pepper in a food processor. With the machine running, slowly pour in the olive oil, then add the basil, and mix until all the ingredients are finely chopped. (If you plan on keeping your pesto for a few days, squeeze just a touch of lemon juice into the mix to keep it a vibrant green.)

- To serve the soup, ladle into a bowl and top with a spoonful of pesto.

FENUGREEK FRIED BREAD

Makes about 16 pieces

MY FATHER USED TO BRING this fried bread home after synagogue, and almost immediately the entire apartment would fill with the earthy aroma. Fenugreek leaves give this bread a robust flavor that rivals the vibrant yellow color. There's no need to add a spread, but if you'd like, try dipping it in yogurt. Fenugreek leaves, while hard to find in stores, can be purchased online.

2 cups all-purpose flour, plus flour for the work surface and dough

3 tablespoons sugar

2 tablespoons dried fenugreek leaves (see Note)

1 tablespoon kosher salt

1 teaspoon ground turmeric

1 tablespoon active dry yeast

¾ cup warm water

Canola oil

- Whisk together 2 cups of the flour, 2 tablespoons of the sugar, the fenugreek leaves, salt, and turmeric in a large bowl. Make a large well in the center of the bowl and add the yeast, remaining 1 tablespoon sugar, and ¼ cup of the warm water. Let the mixture stand until foamy, about 10 minutes.

- Mix together the remaining ½ cup water and 1 tablespoon canola oil in a small bowl and mix it in with the fenugreek mixture. Sprinkle some flour on your work surface, scrape the dough out of the bowl, and knead it until smooth and elastic. Slick another bowl with a little bit of oil and place the dough inside. Cover with a damp cloth and let it rise in a warm place until doubled in size, about 40 minutes.

- Meanwhile, heat 2 inches of oil for frying in a deep skillet or pot. Dust your hands and the work surface with flour. To shape the bread, cut a golf-ball-sized piece from the dough and form it into a disk about the size of your palm. Repeat with the rest of the dough and line up the disks on the floured surface. When the oil is hot enough, gently drop them into the pan one by one. Always work in small batches to keep your oil from getting too cold. Fry the bread for 1 to 2 minutes, turn them over, and cook for another minute, until golden brown.

Note: If you can't find fenugreek leaves at a Middle Eastern grocery, just use fresh mint, or you can grind a mixture of 1 tablespoon fenugreek seeds and 2 tablespoons dried mint.

MOM'S CHICKEN

WITH

POMEGRANATE

AND

WALNUTS

Serves 4 to 6

MY MOM TAUGHT ME A LOT about cooking, but she also taught me about kitchen responsibility—stuff like how to clean rice so there are no black spots and how to properly rinse fava beans. One job I remember in particular was removing, separating, and collecting pomegranate seeds for her famous preserves. This jam goes wonderfully on bread, but mainly it was for her chicken: she'd mix it with water and let it simmer on the chicken inside the pan. It makes a sweet-and sour chicken better than anything you'll find at a Chinese restaurant.

If, for some crazy reason, you manage to live without pomegranate confiture, you can replace it by whisking together $\frac{1}{2}$ cup pomegranate molasses, $\frac{1}{2}$ cup pomegranate juice, and $\frac{1}{4}$ cup honey.

2 pounds chicken thighs and drumsticks
1 tablespoon plus 1 teaspoon kosher salt
2 teaspoons freshly ground black pepper
2 teaspoons ground cumin
2 teaspoons ground turmeric
3 tablespoons canola oil
1$\frac{1}{4}$ cups Pomegranate Confiture (page 273)
3 cups toasted walnuts
Pinch of saffron threads (optional)

- Place a large pot over medium-high heat for 5 minutes. While the pot is heating, pat the chicken dry and season with the salt, pepper, cumin, and turmeric.

- Add the oil to the pot and add the chicken. Brown the chicken on all sides. Overcrowding the pot will steam the chicken instead of searing it. Add the pomegranate confiture and stir in the walnuts and the saffron.

- Place a lid on the pot and bring to a boil, then lower the heat to simmer for 45 minutes. Uncover and reduce the sauce for another 45 minutes. Remove from the heat and take the pot straight to the table for a family-style meal.

COLD EGGPLANT SALAD

Serves 4 to 6

THIS DISH CALLS FOR AN unusually large amount of garlic. The salad is best the day after you've made it, once the flavors have had a chance to marry. The vinegar preserves it—in a way, this recipe is similar to a pickle—so you can enjoy it up to a week later. In fact, the longer you wait, the better it is.

3 large eggplants, stem end trimmed
Kosher salt
Canola oil for frying
1 cup distilled white vinegar
5 garlic cloves, thinly sliced
¼ cup coarsely chopped fresh dill
1½ tablespoons sugar
¼ teaspoon chile flakes

- Slice the eggplant into 1-inch-thick rounds and sprinkle generously with salt. Place them in a colander and let them sit for 45 to 60 minutes. The salt will help purge the excess water and bitterness from the eggplant, so be sure to place a dish underneath the colander if it's not in the sink. Pat the eggplant slices dry with paper towels.

- Heat 1 inch of oil in a deep skillet until the temperature reaches about 375°F. Fry the eggplant until golden brown, about 7 minutes. I suppose you could grill or broil them in the oven as a healthier option, but that's for another chapter. Remove the eggplant with a slotted spoon and place them on a few sheets of paper towel to drain the excess oil.

- Whisk together the vinegar, garlic, dill, sugar, and chile in a large bowl. Slice the eggplant into 1-inch cubes and add them to the bowl. Toss all the ingredients together to coat evenly. Place the salad in an airtight container and refrigerate overnight or for at least 6 hours before serving.

SABICH

Serves 4 to 6

THIS TRADITIONAL IRAQI sandwich filled with fried eggplant, Israeli salad, hummus, and hard-boiled eggs is a favorite at Taïm. There are two speculations about where the name *sabich* came from: some people say it's the name of an Iraqi immigrant who brought the recipe to Palestine in the 1930s; others think it's derived from *sabach,* the Arabic term for "morning," because this originated as a morning sandwich. Regardless of where the name originated, it's a brilliant sandwich. The only truly necessary ingredient is *amba;* I provide a recipe, but you can find it at specialty stores or online if you don't have time to make it from scratch. *Amba* is a tangy sauce featuring green mango and fenugreek; its spice is counteracted here by the addition of creamy tahini.

2 large eggplants, stem ends trimmed
Kosher salt
Canola oil for frying
1 cup finely chopped unpeeled cucumber
1 cup finely chopped tomato
3 tablespoons finely chopped fresh parsley
3 tablespoons chopped scallions (optional)
Freshly ground black pepper
4 to 6 pita loaves
My Hubby's Hummus (page 263)
5,000-Year-Old Eggs (page 195) or hard-boiled eggs, thinly sliced
Amba Sauce (recipe follows)
Tahini Sauce (page 218)

- Peel lengthwise strips of skin off the eggplant ¼ inch apart. Slice the eggplant into ¼-inch-thick rounds and generously salt each piece. Place the eggplant in a colander and allow the excess water to drain for about 1 hour.

- Heat ¼ inch of oil in a deep skillet until the temperature reaches about 375°F. Pat the eggplant dry with a few sheets of paper towels. Fry the eggplant in the hot oil until golden brown, working in small batches. Drain any excess oil on paper towels and set them aside.

- To make the Israeli salad, toss together the cucumber, tomato, parsley, and scallions until well combined. Season with a little salt and pepper and set aside.

- To assemble the *sabich,* cut an opening at one end of the pita bread to make a pocket. Smear the inside of the pita pocket with hummus, then place a spoonful of the Israeli salad at the bottom. Add one slice of eggplant, a few slices of the egg, and then another spoonful of the Israeli salad. Top it off with another piece of eggplant, a few more slices of egg, a spoonful of amba sauce, and some tahini.

- If you have any eggplant left over, cut it up and make Cold Eggplant Salad (page 214) or slather some tahini on it. You can never have too much eggplant.

AMBA SAUCE

You'll need to start this delicious sauce five days ahead, but the results are worth it. We use yellow mangoes instead of the traditional green, since green are harder to find.

6 large yellow mangoes
¼ cup plus 2 tablespoons kosher salt
⅓ cup plus 3 tablespoons canola oil
1 medium yellow onion, finely chopped
¾ cup mustard seeds
¼ cup cumin seeds
2 tablespoons sweet Hungarian paprika
1 tablespoon ground fenugreek
1 tablespoon plus 1 teaspoon ground turmeric
3 teaspoons coriander seeds
12 garlic cloves, finely chopped
½ cup white wine vinegar

- Peel the mangoes and cut them into strips about the size of your pinky. Salt them thoroughly and place them in a large canning jar or glass baking dish. Cover tightly and allow to ferment for 5 days, preferably in the hot sun.

- After 5 days, drain the mangoes in a colander and reserve the juices for later. Scatter the mangoes on a large baking sheet and allow them to dry for 4 to 5 hours.

- Heat 3 tablespoons of canola oil in a large pot over medium heat. Add the onion and sauté until golden brown, about 7 minutes. Add the mustard seeds, cumin seeds, paprika, fenugreek, turmeric, coriander seeds, and garlic. Sauté for another 2 minutes, then add the reserved mango juices. Bring to a simmer, then remove from the heat. Stir in the vinegar and mangoes until well combined. Cool the mixture to room temperature.

- Place the mangoes in a food processor and pulse just until the mangoes are finely chopped. You're looking for a chunky sauce rather than a puree. Transfer the *amba* sauce to a jar with a tight-fitting lid and top off with the remaining ⅓ cup oil. This sauce will keep in your refrigerator for at least 6 months.

Makes about 5 cups

TAHINI SAUCE

½ cup tahini
½ cup water
⅓ cup fresh lemon juice
1 garlic clove
2 teaspoons kosher salt

• Combine the tahini, water, lemon juice, garlic, and salt in a food processor. Puree the mixture until smooth and creamy. Add more liquid if you prefer your tahini sauce to be a little bit runny, then set aside until ready to use.

Makes about 1½ cups

ROASTED RAINBOW BELL PEPPER SALAD

Serves 4 to 6

WHEN MY MOTHER MAKES THIS, it looks so easy to prepare—but then I make it and am reminded how tricky it can be. If you use the best peppers you can find, sweet and fresh, you won't need much of anything else. Add dabs of honey, salt, vinegar, and thyme to accentuate the sweet and tart flavors.

1 large red bell pepper
1 large green bell pepper
1 large orange bell pepper
1 large yellow bell pepper
3 tablespoons honey
1 tablespoon red wine vinegar
¼ teaspoon sweet Hungarian paprika
½ teaspoon kosher salt
Pinch of freshly ground black pepper

- Preheat the broiler on the oven.

- Place the bell peppers on a baking sheet and broil until the skin is charred, about 20 minutes. Remove the tray from the oven and let the peppers cool for 5 minutes. Alternatively, roast the peppers one by one directly on the burner; use tongs to rotate each pepper until all sides are charred, about 5 minutes.

- Place the peppers in a resealable plastic bag for another 20 minutes. This makes it easier to peel off the skin.

- While the bell peppers are in the bag, combine the honey, vinegar, paprika, salt, and pepper in a medium bowl. Whisk together until thoroughly mixed.

- Remove the peppers from the bag and peel away the charred skin. Discard the seeds and stems. Cut the peppers into thin, long strips and toss in the bowl with the honey mixture. Mix together to coat the peppers evenly with the dressing. Serve at room temperature.

SAMBUSAK

Makes about 16 pastries

THIS IS ONE OF MY MOM'S specialties. Think of it as an Israeli version of an empanada, except with a vegetarian filling: dough filled with mashed chickpeas, caramelized onions, and spices, all folded like an empanada and then pan fried. Because of the longer-than-average prep time, it's not an everyday treat.

DOUGH

3 cups all-purpose flour, plus flour for kneading and rolling

1½ tablespoons kosher salt

1½ teaspoons sugar

1 teaspoon active dry yeast

1¼ cups warm water

Canola oil for deep frying, plus oil for the bowl

FILLING

¾ cup dried chickpeas, soaked in cold water overnight

3 tablespoons olive oil

2 medium yellow onions, finely chopped

1 garlic clove, finely chopped

1 tablespoon kosher salt

1 teaspoon ground cumin

1 teaspoon ground turmeric

½ teaspoon chile flakes

Pinch of freshly ground black pepper

Tzatziki (recipe follows)

For the Dough

- Whisk together the flour, salt, and sugar in a large bowl. Create a well in the center of the bowl and add the yeast and warm water. Let the mixture stand until the yeast mixture is foamy, about 10 minutes.

- Use your hands to mix the dough together, and when the dough becomes too sticky to handle, dust your work surface with flour and dump the dough on top. Add a little flour to your hands and knead the dough for a few minutes, then shape it into a ball. Place the dough in another bowl slicked with a little canola oil. Place a damp towel over the bowl and let it rise in a warm place until doubled in size, about 30 minutes.

- Sprinkle a little more flour over your work surface and roll out the dough until about ¼ inch thick. Use a 3-inch round cookie cutter to cut rounds. Place the rounds on a floured baking sheet until ready to assemble.

For the Filling

- Boil the chickpeas until very soft, 40 to 60 minutes, then drain thoroughly. Heat a large skillet over medium heat, then

add the oil and heat it. Add the onions and sauté until caramelized, about 30 minutes. Add the garlic and chickpeas and
cook for another 10 minutes. Add the salt, cumin, turmeric,
chile flakes, and pepper and sauté for 5 minutes. Remove
from the heat and let cool for 15 minutes. Mash the filling
using a potato masher or a fork, then set aside.

To Finish

- Place a spoonful of filling at the center of each round of dough
  and fold the dough over the filling, creating a half moon. Use
  your fingers to pinch the dough closed all around the curved
  edge; there's really no need to use water or an egg wash to
  seal it because the dough is plenty sticky. Line up the pastries on a baking sheet dusted with flour.

- Heat a deep skillet with enough oil to deep-fry the *sambusak*. When the oil reaches a temperature of about 375°F, use
  a slotted spoon to slowly place two or three *sambusak* into
  the skillet. Cook them until golden brown, about 30 seconds
  on each side. Place them on a few paper towels to absorb any
  excess oil.

- Serve the *sambusak* piping-hot with a side of tzatziki.

TZATZIKI

1½ cups yogurt
2 tablespoons olive oil
2 teaspoons fresh lemon juice
⅓ cup finely chopped unpeeled cucumber
½ garlic clove, finely chopped
1½ tablespoons finely chopped fresh mint
1½ teaspoons kosher salt
Pinch of freshly ground black pepper

- Combine all the ingredients in a large bowl and whisk until
  thoroughly mixed. Keep the tzatziki chilled until ready to use.
  It's best used that day, but can be stored in the refrigerator for
  up to 3 days.

Makes about 2 cups

FALAFEL

Makes about 15 balls

THIS IS THE RECIPE THAT HAS led the media to proclaim me the queen of New York falafel. I know this sounds arrogant, but I never much liked falafel until I opened Taïm and developed this recipe. **My version does without the baking powder, baking soda, flour, and bread typically used in other falafel balls. It's a somewhat complicated recipe; though I make it without a meat grinder, I suggest you use one if you can. It makes for a better texture. If you don't like black olives, skip them and grind parsley and cilantro as an alternative.**

2 cups dried chickpeas, soaked in cold water overnight
Canola oil for deep frying
1 medium yellow onion, coarsely chopped
3 garlic cloves, coarsely chopped
1 tablespoon coriander seeds
1 cup pitted Kalamata olives
1½ teaspoons kosher salt
½ teaspoon ground cumin
½ teaspoon freshly ground black pepper

- Drain the chickpeas into a colander. Heat a medium pot filled with enough oil for deep frying.

- Combine the onion and garlic in a food processor. Pulse until the mixture is finely ground. Crush the coriander seeds with the back of a metal spoon. Add them and the chickpeas to the food processor and pulse just until the chickpeas are broken into smaller chunks.

- Add the olives, salt, cumin, and pepper. Process until the mixture is finely chopped but not pureed, scraping down the sides of the container as needed. You're looking for the mixture to resemble coarse meal and not hummus! If the mixture is a little too wet, simply drain off any excess liquid after you pulse it in the food processor. Shape the mixture into 1½-inch balls and set aside.

- When the oil in the pot reaches 375°F, cook 3 to 4 falafel balls at a time until golden brown, about 3 minutes. Make sure to work in small batches to keep your oil nice and hot, which keeps your falafel tender and crispy.

BAKLAVA

Makes about 28 pieces

YOU'LL FIND THIS DESSERT all over the Middle East and as far away as Turkey and Greece. You can get baklava anywhere in Israel, but my mother insists on making hers from scratch. Why? Because store-bought baklava is essentially dunked in honey and syrups; my mother's, meanwhile, is crisp and only moderately sweet, exactly the way I like it. The cardamom is my favorite addition—it lends such a uniquely Middle Eastern taste.

ROSE SYRUP
1 cup water

2 cups sugar

¼ cup honey

One 3-inch strip orange zest

1 cardamom pod

¼ teaspoon rose water

BAKLAVA
6 tablespoons (¾ stick) unsalted butter, melted

¼ cup plus 2 tablespoons canola oil

2 cups raw unsalted peanuts (about 8 ounces)

2 cups pistachios (about 8 ounces)

2 cups walnuts (about 8 ounces)

½ cup powdered sugar

1 teaspoon rose water

⅛ teaspoon ground cardamom (seeds from about 2 pods)

½ teaspoon ground cinnamon

One 16-ounce package frozen phyllo dough, thawed

For the Syrup

- Combine the water, sugar, honey, orange zest, and cardamom pod in a medium saucepan. Simmer over low heat until the sugar is completely dissolved. Remove from the heat, stir in the rose water, and then discard the orange zest and cardamom pod. Transfer the syrup to an airtight container and chill in the refrigerator. The syrup can be made 1 day in advance.

For the Baklava

- Line a 9-by-13-inch baking sheet with parchment paper.

- Stir together the butter and oil in a large bowl. Keep it close to your work area.

- Combine the nuts, powdered sugar, rose water, cardamom, and cinnamon in a food processor. Pulse until finely chopped and almost pasty.

- Preheat the oven to 350°F.

- Place one sheet of phyllo dough on the lined baking sheet. (Keep the unused sheets of phyllo covered with a damp towel as you work.) Trim off the ends if necessary or simply fold it

over to fit the tray. Generously, and I mean generously, brush the top of the phyllo dough with the butter mixture. Place another single layer on top and brush it again. Repeat the process until you have 8 layers of buttery phyllo dough.

- Spread the entire nut mixture on top and firmly pack it down. Place another single layer of phyllo dough on top and brush it with the butter mixture. Repeat the process until you have another 8 layers with the top layer brushed generously.

- Cut the baklava into small diamonds or squares about 2 inches square using a very sharp knife. Lay a sheet of parchment paper on top and bake for 30 minutes. Remove the parchment paper and bake until golden brown, about 15 minutes.

To Serve

- Remove from the oven and immediately pour the chilled rose syrup over the baklava, allowing the syrup to flow into all the crevices. Let it cool completely before serving.

CREAM-BO

Makes about 16 pieces

THIS IS MY VERSION OF THE Krembo, a classic Israeli childhood snack. As kids, we'd get a box of twenty-four Krembos with a cookie base. We'd start eating away, and smearing these chocolate-covered marshmallow treats onto one another's faces. There are different ways to eat a Krembo—some devour the entire chocolate shell first; others hollow out the chocolate by sucking out the creamy inside. I think the best way is on your own, without sharing. You can find them in supermarkets all over Israel, but they taste even better when homemade. If you're short on time (and long on children), you can use store-bought cookies as your base instead of making your own.

HOMEMADE COOKIES
2 cups graham cracker crumbs (about 10 cookies)
8 tablespoons (1 stick) cold unsalted butter, cut into small cubes
¼ cup finely chopped pecans

CREAM FILLING
1 cup sugar
⅓ cup water
½ teaspoon fresh lemon juice
4 egg whites
Pinch of cream of tartar

GANACHE
11 ounces 72% cacao chocolate
3 tablespoons canola oil

For the Homemade Cookies

- Preheat the oven to 350°F.

- Combine the graham crackers, butter, and pecans in a food processor. Pulse until the ingredients are well combined and the texture is like grainy sand.

- Line a baking sheet with parchment paper and form 2-inch disks directly on the sheet. I usually grab the cookie cutter and pack in a little bit of the graham cracker mixture inside, then pat it down. This gives my cookies a nice uniform shape, but if you don't have anything on hand, there are no strict rules against making them freehand.

- Bake in the oven until the cookies are crisp, about 20 minutes. Place them on a rack and cool completely before handling. Reserve the baking sheet and parchment paper to use for assembling the cream-bo.

For the Cream Filling

- Place the sugar, water, and lemon juice in a small saucepan and dissolve completely over low heat. Simmer just until a candy thermometer reads 235°F; alternatively, to check whether the sugar is ready, old-school style, simply scoop a teeny tiny amount of syrup onto a spoon and drop it into an ice bath. If the syrup congeals, it's ready.

Continued

- While the sugar is heating, whip the egg whites with an electric mixer until foamy. Add the cream of tartar and keep whipping over medium speed. Once the syrup is ready, carefully and slowly drizzle the syrup into the mixing bowl with the egg whites while the mixer is running. Keep whipping the whites until the mixing bowl is cool to the touch and the mixture is stiff and glossy, 5 to 7 minutes.

To Assemble

- Scrape the cream filling into a pastry bag fitted with a ½-inch round tip. Place the cookies back on the baking sheet lined with the parchment paper. Carefully pipe a 3-inch mound of cream filling onto each cookie, covering the entire surface area and finishing it off with a peak at the top. Place the almost-finished cream-bo in the freezer overnight or for at least 5 hours.

For the Ganache

- When the cream-bo is finished hanging out in the freezer, you can start on the ganache. Bring a medium pot of water to a simmer. Combine the chocolate and oil in a large bowl, then place it over the simmering water. Melt the chocolate and stir occasionally with a rubber spatula until thoroughly combined.

To Finish

- The next step is a bit messy because it requires you to cover each cookie entirely in chocolate. Delicious but messy. The simplest way is to place a rack on top of the baking sheet lined with parchment paper and then place the cream-bo right on top of that rack. When you pour the ganache over the cream-bo, the ganache will drip past the cooling rack and onto the parchment paper. The ganache should harden almost on contact with the frozen cream-bo, creating a nice chocolate shell. Use a spatula to lift the cookies from the cooling rack and onto a serving platter. Crumple up the parchment paper for an easy cleanup so you can have more time to enjoy these gooey treats.

FANCY-SCHMANCY

RESTAURANT-WORTHY DISHES

Time for a confession.

When I first opened Taïm, my falafel restaurant in Greenwich Village, I felt a slight twinge of shame.

THESE DAYS TAÏM IS successful beyond my wildest dreams. *The New Yorker* proclaimed it "elating," and *Zagat* called it "bliss in a pita." But back at the beginning...

There I was, a graduate of the top cooking school in Israel, a veteran of the finest restaurants in New York, including Bolo, Danube, and Tabla under the tutelage of David Bouley and Bobby Flay. And then finally, nine years and God only knows how much sweat and tears later, I fulfill a lifelong dream and open my very own restaurant, right here in New York City, capital of the world's finest cuisine! And what do I open?

A falafel place.

Really?

I imagined how my friends in Israel would react:

"Mah—stahm falafel? Nothing but a stupid falafel joint?"

Falafel is ethnic and unique here in the States, but in Israel falafel stands are a shekel a dozen. I'm not exaggerating when I say that just about every city block in Tel Aviv has at least one falafel place and often two or three. They're ubiquitous, they're indistinguishable, and they're typically run by some sixty-year-old man with a raspy cigarette voice and a gold chain around his neck who doesn't know parsley from paprika, let alone Bolo from Bouley.

So to train and work for ten years only to open a falafel joint—well, it's kind of like getting an MBA from Harvard, interning with Warren Buffett, slaving through seven years of eighty-hour workweeks at Goldman Sachs, and then opening a 7-Eleven.

At least that's how I felt.

Why am I telling you this? First, because there's a lesson here: that to succeed you have to be true to who you are. I suppose I could have opened a jacket-required, $400-per-bottle-of-wine bistro in midtown Manhattan with snappy white tablecloths and a maître d' in a form-fitting suit, the kind of place where you can't get a reservation less than six months in advance unless you're a Knick or a Yankee. But if I'd opened that kind of restaurant, I never could have succeeded the way I have with Taïm, because it just wouldn't have been me. To the extent that Taïm is beloved, it's got a bit to do with my falafel recipe and a lot to do with the fact that at Taïm everything from the food to the color of the aprons perfectly reflects who I am.

Not that I ever gave up on my dream of going upscale. But during the five years in which I was growing Taïm into a Manhattan staple, my dream of opening an upscale restaurant changed. I must have visited a couple hundred restaurants during the years of Taïm's infancy—not just to observe and learn but because eating in restaurants is my hobby. And after all those visits and countless five-course meals, I decided that if I ever opened another restaurant, I'd want it to be fancy but not *too* fancy. Because if it's too formal, customers come in with a rigid expectation of what the experience will be like. They expect a certain kind of dish, served on a certain kind of plate, by a certain kind of waiter. And while I didn't doubt that I could meet expectations, I feared that in the process my creativity would be stifled. And another thing—a perfectly coiffed restaurant puts a lot of effort into décor that I don't feel comfortable with. I'm not the kind of lady who can sit comfortably at a table dressed in crisp white linen. So I prefer to concentrate on what I do best—flavor.

Thus Balaboosta was born. And while it may not be the fanciest restaurant in New York, it's as fancy as I want to go. In other words, it's fancy-schmancy—my way of saying that even though there is a great wine list and I care deeply about the presentation of the food on the plates, I don't take the fanciness too seriously.

Tackle the recipes in this chapter when you've got some time on your hands. If these dishes have one thing in common, it's that they go beyond the boundaries of typical home cooking (think seared duck breast and grilled octopus) and therefore require more time and effort than the others in this book. It also helps if you've got a strong motivation to impress your friends. But don't let their praise (and there *will be* praise; trust me) go to your head—after all, it's just fancy-schmancy.

EGGPLANT SLATHERED

WITH

TAHINI, LEMON,

AND

HERB SALAD

Serves 4

THIS DISH IS ABOUT LAYERS OF flavor—the smokiness of the eggplant (which can be burned on an open flame, roasted in the oven, or grilled), the creaminess of the tahini, and the freshness of the mint, parsley, cilantro, and lemon. It works great as an appetizer, passed hors d'oeuvre, or a snack slathered on bread.

If you have date molasses or honey on hand, drizzle a few drops on top for a little sweetness.

2 large eggplant
½ **cup chopped fresh cilantro**
½ **cup chopped fresh parsley**
½ **cup chopped fresh mint**
½ **red chile, such as red jalapeño or a long red chile, cored, seeded, and cut into long, thin strips**
1 lemon, segmented, with 1 tablespoon juice
Kosher salt
Freshly ground black pepper
½ **cup Tahini Sauce (page 218)**

- Cut the eggplant in half lengthwise. Place the eggplant cut sides down on a large nonstick skillet, then place a sheet of aluminum foil on top. Put another skillet on top and roast in the pan over medium heat until tender, 20 to 30 minutes.

- While the eggplant is roasting, toss together the cilantro, parsley, mint, chile, lemon segments, and lemon juice in a large bowl and season with salt and pepper to taste.

- When the eggplant is cooked, remove from the heat and discard the foil. Slather the eggplant with the tahini sauce and top with the herb salad.

SUNCHOKE SOUP

WITH

CRISPY CHESTNUTS

Serves 3 to 4

THIS RECIPE ONCE WON ME A trophy. I was representing Israel in a chef competition sponsored by the U.S. embassy and created this delicate soup as my entry. It might not be easy to get your hands on sunchokes (also known as Jerusalem artichokes), but it's worth a try. They're starchy and sweet, almost acting like cream. Earthy and crunchy chestnuts are a great complement. You can find peeled chestnuts in a bag just about anywhere.

If you need to avoid dairy products, substitute 2 more cups water for the whole milk.

2 tablespoons unsalted butter

3 tablespoons canola oil

1 medium yellow onion, coarsely chopped

1 leek, white parts only, finely chopped

2 garlic cloves, coarsely chopped

1 medium carrot, cut in half

2 pounds sunchokes, peeled and coarsely chopped

2 fresh thyme sprigs

1½ tablespoons kosher salt

¼ teaspoon freshly ground black pepper

¼ cup dry white wine

2 cups whole milk

2 cups water

5 chestnuts, coarsely chopped

2 tablespoons heavy cream

- Melt the butter with 1 tablespoon of the canola oil in a medium pot over medium-high heat. Add the onion and leek and sauté until soft, about 5 minutes. Add the garlic, carrot, sunchokes, and thyme and season with the salt and pepper. Sauté the vegetables until soft and fragrant, about 10 minutes.

- Add the white wine and deglaze the pot. Reduce until about half, then add the milk and water. Lower the heat and simmer for 30 to 45 minutes.

- While the soup is simmering, heat a small skillet with the remaining 2 tablespoons oil and fry the chestnuts until crispy, about 3 minutes. Drain them on paper towels and set aside.

- Remove the soup from the heat and allow to cool for 20 minutes. Discard the carrots and thyme. Place the sunchoke soup and heavy cream in a blender and puree until smooth. Adjust the seasonings if needed.

- Reheat the soup over medium heat and serve with the crispy chestnuts on top.

GRILLED OCTOPUS

WITH

MICROGREENS

AND

BLOOD ORANGES

Serves 4 to 6

OCTOPUS IS A VERY DELICATE seafood that takes a while to prepare. You begin by tenderizing it—which takes 2$\frac{1}{2}$ hours. The good news is that most of that time it's just sitting in the oven. After that, a quick grill creates the perfect charred flavor you're looking for, which is brilliant for the texture of the octopus. The simple marinade is my version of sweet and sour—the sumac is tangy, the orange a bit sweet.

Kosher salt

3 pounds octopus

$\frac{1}{4}$ cup plus 2 tablepoons olive oil

5 garlic cloves

3 fresh thyme sprigs

1 fresh rosemary sprig

1 bay leaf

1 cup blood orange juice or just the regular stuff

2 tablespoons sumac (see **Note**)

2 tablespoons canola oil

$\frac{1}{2}$ cup fresh parsley

MICROGREEN AND BLOOD ORANGE SALAD

1 blood orange

2 teaspoons olive oil

Pinch of kosher salt

Pinch of freshly ground black pepper

4 cups microgreens (any variety will do)

$\frac{1}{2}$ small fennel bulb, cored and thinly shaved

Harissa Oil (optional; page **253**)

- Preheat the oven to 275°F.

- Bring a large pot of salted water to a boil. While the water is heating, prepare a large bowl of ice water and set it aside. Dunk the octopus into the boiling water and cook for about 5 minutes. Use a pair of tongs to transfer the octopus directly into the ice bath and cool completely.

- Cut the octopus into 3-inch pieces and place in a Dutch oven or other large, heavy pot. Add $\frac{1}{4}$ cup of the olive oil, 3 of the garlic cloves, the thyme, rosemary, and bay leaf and toss to combine with the octopus. Place the lid on the Dutch oven and cook in the oven until tender, about 2 hours (when you stick a fork in the thickest part of a tentacle and it comes out easily, the octopus is ready). Remove from the oven and cool completely.

- While the octopus is in the oven, prepare the marinade by combining the remaining 2 garlic cloves, the blood orange juice, sumac, 2 teaspoons salt, the canola oil, the remaining 2 tablespoons olive oil, and the parsley in a food processor or blender. Pulse until all the ingredients are finely chopped. Pour the blood orange juice mixture over the octopus after it has cooled. Transfer to an airtight container and marinate, refrigerated, for at least 1 hour and up to overnight.

- Remove the octopus from the refrigerator and bring it to room temperature. Get your grill nice and hot or heat up a cast-iron skillet on the stovetop.

- While the grill is heating, cut the blood orange into segments. The fancy-schmancy way is to trim the ends of the blood orange so that it stands on its own. With a sharp fillet or paring knife, and starting from the top of the orange, slowly slice off the skin and the pith by following the curve of the orange. You know you're doing this right when you've sliced off just enough pith to expose the pulp of the orange. Repeat this process until you have a naked orange. Next hold the orange with one hand over a bowl and take the paring knife in the other hand. Carefully extract each individual segment by sliding your knife between the pulp and the connective membrane on both sides. Pop out the segment and throw it into the bowl under your hand and repeat the process for the remaining orange. Leave about 1 teaspoon of the juices that dripped into the bowl and discard the rest. Hold the segments to one side of the bowl and quickly whisk in the oil, salt, and pepper.

- When the grill is ready, char all the octopus pieces for about a minute on each side. Remove from the heat and arrange them on a serving platter. Add the microgreens and fennel to the orange segments and toss lightly to coat evenly. Use your hands to delicately place a tall mound of the salad on top of the octopus and serve immediately.

- If you'd like to step up the fancy-schmancy level, serve the octopus on individual serving plates, place a tall mound of salad on each, and drizzle the edges of the plate with harissa oil.

Note: If you can't find sumac at a Middle Eastern market, whip up your own substitute by mixing 1 tablespoon lemon zest with $\frac{1}{2}$ teaspoon sweet Hungarian paprika.

PAN-SEARED DUCK BREAST

WITH

CIDER

AND

MUSTARD SEEDS

Serves 4 to 6

WHEN I FIRST CAME TO THE United States and began working in kitchens, I survived on an extremely tight budget. To make ends meet, I ate Peking duck on rice every day, which was amazing because I'd probably had duck only once or twice in my life before. Nowhere else could I find such a tasty and fulfilling meal for only $3.25. It's safe to say that I developed a fond feeling for this bird and started to experiment with it on my own. As this recipe suggests, I especially like sweet, spicy, and tangy flavors with duck.

3 tablespoons unsalted butter

$\frac{1}{2}$ McIntosh apple, peeled, cored, and cut into small cubes

1 tablespoon mustard seeds

2 teaspoons finely chopped fresh rosemary

$\frac{1}{2}$ small red chile, such as red jalapeño or a long red chile, cored, seeded, and finely chopped

1 teaspoon Dijon mustard

1 cup apple cider

Four 6-ounce boneless duck breasts

$1\frac{1}{2}$ teaspoons kosher salt

$\frac{1}{2}$ teaspoon freshly ground black pepper

- Melt 2 tablespoons of the butter in a medium saucepan. Add the apple, mustard seeds, rosemary, and red chile. Sauté until the apple is tender, then add the Dijon mustard and apple cider. Bring the mixture to a boil, then lower the heat and simmer until reduced by half. Remove the sauce from the heat and stir in the remaining 1 tablespoon butter. Keep warm until ready to use.

- Preheat the oven to 400°F.

- Heat a large ovenproof skillet over high heat for 10 minutes. Meanwhile, score the skin of the duck breasts in a cross-hatch pattern about $\frac{1}{4}$ inch deep. Season both sides with salt and pepper. When the pan is hot, hot, hot, place the duck skin side down and sear until brown and crispy, about 5 minutes. Flip the duck breasts and place the skillet in the oven. Bake for 6 minutes with the skin side up, then remove from the oven and allow the duck breasts to rest for 10 minutes.

- When ready to serve, slice the duck at a 45-degree angle. Ladle on a spoonful of the cider sauce and devour immediately.

HOMEMADE SPINACH FETTUCCINE

WITH

RICOTTA

AND

WALNUT QUENELLES

Serves 4 to 6

LIKE ANY DOUGH, FRESH PASTA requires lots of care and attention. The spinach adds an element of healthfulness, and the ricotta is creamy. This recipe is for fettuccine, but the sauce also works with cavatelli or any shapes you can master.

By the way, kale will work here as well as spinach.

HOMEMADE SPINACH PASTA

¼ cup kosher salt

4 cups packed spinach leaves

5 large eggs

4 cups all-purpose flour, plus flour for the work surface and dusting

3 tablespoons olive oil

2 tablespoons water

RICOTTA AND WALNUT QUENELLES

1 cup walnuts

8 to 10 garlic cloves

¾ cup canola oil

½ cup ricotta

2 tablespoons olive oil

¼ cup coarsely chopped sun-dried tomatoes

1 leek, white and light green parts only, sliced into thin strips

Kosher salt

For the Spinach Pasta

- Bring a medium pot of water with 3 tablespoons of the salt to a boil. Have a bowl of ice water handy. Add the spinach and cook for 1 minute. Drain the spinach and transfer to the ice bath to cool completely. This will preserve the bright green color for your homemade pasta. Drain the spinach one more time and lay it out on dish towels; squeeze out any excess water. Transfer the spinach to a blender and add 1 of the eggs. Puree until smooth. Set aside.

- Using an electric stand mixer on low speed, combine the flour and the remaining 4 eggs. Add the remaining 1 tablespoon salt, the olive oil, water, and finally the spinach puree. Mix thoroughly, then remove the dough from the bowl. Shape it into a large ball and wrap the dough in plastic wrap. Reserve it at room temperature for 30 minutes.

- Divide the dough into four pieces and work with one piece at a time, keeping the rest of the dough covered so it doesn't dry out. If you have a pasta machine, roll out the dough into a thin sheet—I wouldn't say paper-thin, more like three-sheets-of-paper-thin (if your pasta machine has numbered positions, use 1¾). Otherwise, lightly flour your work surface and roll out the dough into a rectangular sheet.

- To make the fettuccine, loosely roll the sheet into a log. Use a very sharp knife to cut the log into ¼-inch-thick strips. Unroll the cut pieces, lightly dust them with flour, and toss into a bowl.

- Repeat this process with the remaining dough.

For the Ricotta and Walnut Quenelles

- Place the walnuts in a food processor and pulse until finely chopped. Transfer to a small bowl.

- Place the garlic cloves in the food processor and pulse until finely chopped. Transfer to another small bowl.

- Heat the canola oil in a deep skillet over medium-low heat. Add the garlic and cook until golden brown, but be careful not to burn it! Add the walnuts and remove from the heat, stirring frequently until cooled completely. Drain thoroughly and combine the walnut mixture with the ricotta. Use a spoon to form football-shaped quenelles and set aside.

To Finish

- Bring a large pot of salted water to a boil and cook the pasta until tender, 2 to 3 minutes. Drain the pasta.

- When ready to serve, heat the 2 tablespoons olive oil in a large skillet over medium-high heat. Add the sun-dried tomatoes and leek and sauté just until soft and fragrant, about 4 minutes. Toss in the cooked pasta and toss evenly to coat. Season with salt and top off the dish with the ricotta and walnut quenelles.

SHRIMP KATAIF

Serves 4 to 6

THIS DISH HAS FOLLOWED ME for ten years. I've contemplated rotating it off the menu at Balaboosta, but the truth is, my customers adore it. *Kataif* means "shredded phyllo"—it's usually found in Middle Eastern pastries, but here I use it to wrap the shrimp, to give it a crust. What makes the dish so good? The combination of the crust's texture and the sauce melding fresh aioli, ginger juice, and wasabi-flavored tobiko. It looks complicated, but you'll be surprised by how easy it is.

WASABI TOBIKO SAUCE
One 4-inch piece fresh ginger, peeled and coarsely chopped
2 tablespoons water
1 large egg
1½ cups canola oil
1½ teaspoons kosher salt
1 teaspoon sugar
1 teaspoon sambal
1 tablespoon finely chopped scallion, white part only
½ of a 1-pound wasabi tobiko package

SHRIMP KATAIF
½ of a 1-pound *kataif* package, thawed and kept moist under a damp cloth
1 pound large tiger shrimp, peeled and deveined
Canola oil for frying

For the Wasabi Tobiko Sauce

- Combine the ginger and water in a food processor and puree until smooth. Drain in a fine-mesh sieve and reserve the ginger juice, discarding the solids left in the sieve.

- Add the egg to the food processor and, while the machine is running, slowly drizzle in the canola oil until you get a smooth, creamy consistency. Transfer the mixture to a mixing bowl and stir in the salt, sugar, ginger juice, sambal, and scallion. Adjust the seasonings if needed. Add the tobiko and stir to combine. You should have about 2 cups sauce.

For the Shrimp Kataif

- Measure out thin strands of *kataif* about 4 inches long and wrap each shrimp starting from the tail end. Place a damp cloth over the shrimp *kataif* until you're ready to cook them.

- Heat 1 inch of canola oil in a deep skillet until the temperature is about 375°F. Carefully fry the shrimp until golden brown on both sides, about 4 minutes. Drain the shrimp on a few paper towels.

- Serve warm with the tobiko sauce.

FLUKE CEVICHE

WITH

BEETS

AND

FENNEL

Serves 4 to 6

AT BALABOOSTA WE OFFER A ceviche special that changes every day. I alternate between fluke, arctic char, salmon, and tuna, plus a few others. Ceviche is a playful dish, and this recipe is one of my favorite results. The raw beets that get mixed with the ceviche add crunch, the orange provides the sweetness and citrus, and the fennel spices it up.

This recipe works just as well with salmon.

3 tablespoons fresh lime juice
1 teaspoon sugar
1/2 teaspoon kosher salt
1/2 pound skinless fluke fillet, cut into small cubes
1 small beet, peeled and sliced into matchsticks
2 tablespoons very thinly shaved fennel
2 tablespoons finely chopped red onion
4 orange segments, cut into small pieces
1/2 small jalapeño chile, cored, seeded, and finely chopped
3 tablespoons finely chopped fresh cilantro
Toasted pistachios, coarsely chopped
Microgreens (optional)

- Mix together the lime juice, sugar, and salt in a large bowl. Toss with the fish to combine thoroughly. Then add the beet, fennel, red onion, orange, jalapeño, and cilantro. For a fancy-schmancy presentation, use a ring mold or large round cookie cutter to form the ceviche into a nice circular shape, then top with toasted pistachios and microgreens.

SEARED SNAPPER

WITH

RED PEPPER LEMON SAUCE

AND

RICE CAKES

Serves 4

I ATE A LOT OF SPICY FISH
growing up. The fish my mom used to buy had typically been frozen or farmed fresh, so the focus of the recipe was never on the quality of the catch but on the sauce and spices. This recipe, however, is all about the fish. Freshness and quality are of the utmost importance; the pairings are delicate in flavor. You can also replace snapper with halibut, black bass, red snapper, or grouper—but choose carefully, being sure the fish's eyes are still shiny and the meat bounces back when you poke it.

The sauce is also a lovely complement for chicken or lamb.

RED PEPPER LEMON SAUCE
1 medium red bell pepper, cored, seeded, and coarsely chopped
2 wedges Perfect Preserved Lemons (page **276**), coarsely chopped
2 cloves Roasted Garlic (page **273**)
⅓ cup fresh lemon juice
¼ teaspoon sugar
1½ teaspoons kosher salt
½ teaspoon chile flakes
1¼ cups canola oil

4 snapper fillets
Kosher salt
Freshly ground black pepper
2 tablespoons canola oil
Rice Cakes (recipe follows)
Microgreens

- Combine the bell pepper, preserved lemons, roasted garlic, lemon juice, sugar, salt, and chile flakes in a food processor. Puree until smooth, then slowly drizzle in the 1¼ cups canola oil while the machine is running. Transfer the sauce to an airtight container and refrigerate, bringing it to room temperature before serving. The sauce is best that day, but can be made 1 day in advance.

- Place a large skillet over high heat for 5 minutes. Meanwhile, pat the fish fillets dry, then season both sides with salt and pepper. Add the 2 tablespoons canola oil to the hot skillet and carefully place the fillets skin side down in the pan. Cook for 3 minutes, flip them over, and fry for another 2 minutes.

- To serve, place a spoonful of the red pepper lemon sauce onto one end of the plate and drag the spoon to the opposite side, smearing the sauce across the plate. Place one rice cake over the center, slice each fillet in half, and place both halves on the rice cake. Garnish with some microgreens. Repeat with the other 3 plates.

RICE CAKES

¾ cup sushi rice
1 teaspoon kosher salt
Pinch of saffron threads
¼ cup finely chopped fresh parsley
1 tablespoon finely chopped thyme
1 teaspoon mustard seeds
1 tablespoon dried currants or chopped raisins
¼ cup store-bought fried onions or shallots
All-purpose flour for dusting
Canola oil for deep frying

- Wash the rice thoroughly in cold water and drain. Place in a medium saucepan with 1¼ cups water and the salt. Bring to a boil, then lower the heat to simmer. Cover and cook until tender, 15 to 18 minutes.

- While the rice is cooking, soak the saffron threads in 1 tablespoon of water and set aside. Combine the parsley, thyme, mustard seeds, currants, and fried onions in a large bowl. Add the cooked rice and mix everything together. Add the saffron threads with the soaking liquid and mix thoroughly. Form eight rice patties about 3 inches in diameter and 1½ inches thick. Lightly coat in flour and dust off the excess.

- Add 2 inches of oil to a deep skillet over medium-high heat. Fry the rice cakes until golden brown, 3 to 5 minutes.

Makes 4 cakes

INFUSED OILS

INFUSED OILS ARE AN EASY WAY TO CLASS UP ANY DISH. THEY PROVIDE COLOR, flavor, and fat as needed. And sometimes they're just good for a little decoration. Of course, there are people who think infused oils are passé—but I'll never give them up. Here are three options (though they might inspire you to try others or even to cook with them when just regular oil is called for). The cilantro pairs well with eggplant and ceviche (see pages 236 and 248); the harissa with fried olives (see page 120); and the lemon oil with tabbouleh (see page 145).

LEMON OIL

Makes about 1 cup

Grated zest of 4 lemons
¹⁄₂ teaspoon ground turmeric
1 cup canola oil

- Combine the lemon zest, turmeric, and canola oil in a small saucepan. Bring to a very, very low simmer and cook for 20 minutes. Remove from the heat and allow the oil to cool completely.

- You can strain the oil through a fine-mesh sieve, but personally I like to leave in the zest for added texture. Transfer the oil to a squeeze bottle with a tip large enough to pass the zest. Store in the refrigerator for up to 4 weeks.

HARISSA OIL

Makes about 1 cup

³⁄₄ cup World's Best Harissa (page 272)
1 cup canola oil

- Combine the harissa and oil in a small saucepan and bring to a very low simmer for 30 minutes. Remove from the heat and allow the oil to cool completely.

- Strain the harissa oil through a fine-mesh sieve lined with cheesecloth. And don't even think about throwing away the harissa! Use it in a Spicy Chicken Tagine (page 29) or Casablanca Catch (page 23) to double its use. Stored in a fine-tip squeeze bottle, it can be kept in the refrigerator for up to 4 weeks.

CILANTRO OIL

Makes about 1 cup

3 tablespoons kosher salt
1 large bunch of cilantro, rinsed
½ cup canola oil

- Bring 8 cups water and the salt to a boil in a large pot. Meanwhile, prepare an ice bath for the cilantro by filling a large bowl with ice and cold water.

- When the water comes to a boil, place the cilantro, stems and all, in the pot and leave for 7 seconds. Use a pair of tongs to quickly remove the bunch from the boiling water and plunge it into the ice bath. Blanching the cilantro will give the infused oil a nice bright green color. When it is completely cooled off, drain the cilantro from the ice bath. Squeeze out all the excess water by wrapping the cilantro in a clean dish towel and wringing it as hard as you can. Make sure it's a towel that you don't mind staining green (unless of course you're a master at stain removal, which I am not).

- Combine the cilantro and oil in a blender. Gradually increase the speed of the blender until you reach the maximum level and puree the cilantro until the container for the blender is warm to the touch. Once it reaches this point, puree it for another 3 minutes.

- Line a fine-mesh sieve with cheesecloth and hold it over a bowl. If you can somehow manage to suspend the sieve without holding it, even better! Pour in the cilantro oil mixture and allow the oil to seep through gradually. If you're feeling a little impatient, you can use a rubber spatula to gently push the oil through the sieve, but this will result in a somewhat cloudy infused oil.

- Transfer the cilantro oil to a fine-tip squeeze bottle for an instant fancy-schmancy look. It can be stored in the refrigerator for up to 3 weeks.

BERRIES CRÈME BRÛLÉE

Serves 4

I KNOW THIS ONE TAKES effort and even special equipment, including a torch and ramekins. But once you have them, you'll want to use them again. And I assure you that this recipe will seriously impress your friends. My version differs from traditional crème brûlée because here the berries are folded inside the cream and the proportion of berries to cream ensures a berry with every bite.

2 cups mixed berries
½ cup plus 2 tablespoons sugar, plus sugar for dusting
2½ cups heavy cream
1 vanilla bean, split in half lengthwise, or 1 teaspoon vanilla powder
6 large egg yolks

- Preheat the oven to 325°F.

- Combine the berries and 2 tablespoons of the sugar in a small saucepan. Simmer over medium-low heat until the berries are soft, about 10 minutes. Remove from the heat and set aside.

- While the berries are cooking, combine the heavy cream and vanilla bean in a medium saucepan. Bring to a rapid simmer, then remove from the heat. Cover the saucepan and allow the vanilla to infuse for about 15 minutes.

- Whisk the egg yolks and the remaining ½ cup sugar in a large bowl until well blended and the color turns a pale yellow. Discard the vanilla bean from the heavy cream, then slowly add the cream to the egg yolks, stirring frequently. Gently fold in the berry mixture.

- Pour the mixture into shallow ramekins, about 5 inches in diameter. Place the ramekins in a large cake pan and fill with enough hot water to go halfway up the sides of the ramekins. Bake just until the crème brûlée is almost firm but still jiggling in the middle, 30 to 45 minutes. Allow the crème brûlée to cool completely, then refrigerate for at least 4 hours and up to overnight before serving.

- Remove the crème brûlée from the refrigerator 30 minutes prior to serving. Dust the tops of each ramekin with just enough sugar to form a thin layer over the entire surface. Melt the sugar with a torch until a deep brown color, about 30 seconds.

KANAFEH

Makes 12 pieces

I LIKE TO DESCRIBE *KANAFEH* as Middle Eastern cheesecake. It can be found all over the Middle East, but the best ones need to be sought out. We used to drive for an hour in Israel (akin to driving for five hours in the United States, since Israel is so small) to a town called Dalet El Carmel in the Galilee, up north, to get our favorite *kanafeh.* I can picture those large, round aluminum trays layered with *kanafeh* being kept warm over an open flame, the heavenly smell permeating the entire restaurant.

My version of this famous dessert is less sweet and made with more readily available ingredients, such as semolina and ricotta. The crispiness pairs especially well with pistachio ice cream, so consider serving with that even if it's not the most traditional way to enjoy this dessert.

2 cups whole milk
¼ cup granulated sugar
2 tablespoons plus 2 teaspoons semolina
2 cups ricotta
Grated zest of ½ lemon
1 teaspoon orange blossom water
9 ounces *kataif* (shredded phyllo dough), thawed if frozen
⅓ cup powdered sugar
8 tablespoons (1 stick) unsalted butter, melted, plus butter for the pan
Rose Syrup (page 278)
Chopped pistachios

- Preheat the oven to 325°F.

- Heat the milk and granulated sugar in a medium saucepan just until small bubbles start to appear around the edges. Slowly stir in the semolina until the mixture thickens, then remove from the heat and cool to room temperature. Add the ricotta, lemon zest, and orange blossom water and stir well to combine.

- Place the *kataif* in a large bowl, add the powdered sugar, and use your fingers to toss gently to coat evenly. Drizzle in the melted butter and toss lightly to combine. If you're not moving on to the next step immediately, cover the bowl with a damp cloth to keep the mixture from drying out.

- Grease a 9-by-13-inch baking sheet with butter. Divide the *kataif* in half and lay out the first half evenly on the baking sheet. Spread the ricotta mixture evenly over the entire sheet, then top it off with the remaining *kataif.* If you've made a sandwich before, then this is just a walk in the park.

- Bake the *kanafeh* until golden brown, 15 to 20 minutes. Place the sheet on a rack and cool to room temperature. Cut it into 3-by-3¼-inch pieces, drizzle with the rose syrup and scatter over a small handful of the chopped pistachios. It looks fancy without your having to spend all day in the kitchen.

CAN'T LIVE WITHOUT

BASICS
FOR
EVERYDAY
USE

How do you define a food that you can't live without?

For my dad, it means carrying his favorite home-made hot sauce, *s'chug* (aka Yemenite Dynamite), in a plastic container to restaurants.

———

W E DIDN'T EAT OUT MUCH WHEN I WAS a kid, but the few memories I have are of my father pulling *s'chug* out of his pocket, in full view of the waitstaff, while my siblings and I cringed in embarrassment.

My husband Stefan's addiction to hummus is no less potent—though, thank god, he's a bit better behaved. The day I catch Stefan with hummus on him is the day he says good-bye to me forever.

At Balaboosta, our number one can't-live-without item is probably harissa—the red Tunisian-Moroccan paste that shows up in more than a few recipes in this book. Customers love the smell, the bold flavors, the texture, the spice, to the point where they ask for it by name. My own love of harissa is no less powerful—when I open the jar I've made the night before, it feels like opening a jack-in-the-box—the smell just jumps out and totally engulfs me.

But these days, what I really can't live without is the spicy-sweet adobo rub that I apply to the steak at Balaboosta. The recipe for this rub came to me courtesy of a former boss. The mere thought of meat without adobo makes me want to be vegetarian.

Recipes for each of these sauces, dressings, and sides—plus a few more—appear in the pages ahead. Most of these dishes last for six months or more. So you might set aside a full day to prepare them all and then store them in the fridge so they'll be ready the next time you cook (or feel like stashing some in your pockets).

MY HUBBY'S HUMMUS

Makes about 5 cups

THIS RECIPE BRINGS TO MIND the expression "The student has overtaken the teacher." Six years ago I taught my husband, Stefan, how to make hummus. Since then, Stefan has become nothing less than a hummus freak, tinkering constantly with my original recipe until, finally, his hummus is far superior to my own. All over the world, the ingredients for hummus are the same. It's the proportions that make all the difference—and Stef has cracked the code.

Start the hummus a day ahead of when you intend to use it by soaking the chickpeas overnight.

There are so many more things you can do with the finished product than just smearing it on pita. Add it to sandwiches or make it a meal by layering ground beef, sautéed mushrooms, and hard-boiled eggs on top.

3 cups dried chickpeas
2½ teaspoons baking soda
2 large garlic cloves, finely chopped
⅓ cup tahini (I prefer the White Dove brand)
3½ tablespoons fresh lemon juice
5 tablespoons olive oil
1½ teaspoons kosher salt
½ teaspoon ground cumin
⅛ teaspoon freshly ground black pepper
¼ teaspoon sweet Hungarian paprika, for garnish

- Put the chickpeas and 1½ teaspoons of the baking soda in a bowl. Add cold water to cover and leave to soak overnight.

- Drain the chickpeas and transfer them to a large pot of water. Add the remaining 1 teaspoon baking soda and bring to a boil. Boil until the chickpeas are tender, 45 to 50 minutes. Skim off any floating shells.

- Drain, reserving 1 cup of the cooking liquid, and let the chickpeas cool completely.

- Combine the chickpeas, garlic, reserved liquid (see Note), tahini, lemon juice, 3 tablespoons of the olive oil, salt, cumin, and pepper in a food processor and puree until smooth and creamy.

- When ready to serve, put the hummus on a plate or in a shallow bowl, and garnish with the remaining 2 tablespoons of olive oil and the paprika.

- The hummus can be stored in an airtight container for up to 3 days.

Note: If you forget to reserve the cooking liquid, you can substitute 1 cup ice-cold water. But using the cooking liquid will give the hummus a richer, bolder flavor.

BAHARAT

Makes about 1⅓ cups

IN ARABIC *BAHARAT* MEANS "spices" and refers to a blend of spices. This combination of spices, which can improve even the most inedible dishes, changes from region to region, from one dish to another; its use varies from lamb to fish, from chicken to pickles. Here is the combination of spices I prefer, and I think it goes with everything. I use it in Chamusta (page 95), Sinaya (page 98) and Really-Not-so-Short Ribs (page 188).

2 tablespoons ground black pepper
3 tablespoons allspice
3 tablespoons ground coriander
5 tablespoons ground cinnamon
1 tablespoon ground cloves
3 tablespoons ground cumin
1 teaspoon ground cardamom
4 teaspoons ground nutmeg
2 tablespoons sweet Hungarian paprika
1 tablespoon dried lemon zest (optional)
4 teaspoons dried ginger (optional)

• Combine all the ingredients together until well mixed. Store in an airtight jar and keep away from direct sunlight.

WHAT TICKLES
YOUR PICKLE

IN THE STATES, PEOPLE MOST OFTEN THINK OF PICKLED CUCUMBERS WHEN THEY hear the word *pickles.* **But in Israel, when we say** *hamutzim,* **we refer to all the vegetables that we pickle, including cauliflower, eggplants, carrots, celery, red onions, and beets. Pickling is a terrific way to make use of old vegetables: before they go bad, simply pickle them instead of throwing them out. Until I learned this technique, I had no idea how delicious a pickled cherry tomato could be.**

CUCUMBER

Makes about 1 quart

2½ cups water

1½ cups white vinegar

½ cup sugar

¼ cup kosher salt

1 small yellow onion, thinly sliced

2 garlic cloves, thinly sliced

1 teaspoon mustard seeds

¼ teaspoon ground turmeric

¼ teaspoon dill seeds

6 to 8 Kirby cucumbers, sliced into thin rounds

- Combine the water, vinegar, sugar, and salt in a small pot and bring to a boil. Stir until the sugar is completely dissolved and remove from the heat. Cool to room temperature.

- Mix the onion, garlic, mustard seeds, turmeric, dill seeds, and cucumbers together in a large bowl. When the vinegar mixture has cooled off, pour it over the cucumbers and stir well to combine.

- Transfer the pickles to a 1-quart glass jar and allow them to ferment in the refrigerator for at least 1 week. They will keep for a few months.

CAULIFLOWER

Makes about 2 quarts

2½ cups water
1 cup distilled white vinegar
¾ sugar
1½ tablespoons *amba* spice mix
1 tablespoon kosher salt
Pinch of ground turmeric
1 large head cauliflower
1½ teaspoons nigella seeds (see page 49)
1 garlic clove

- Stir together the water, vinegar, sugar, *amba*, salt, and turmeric in a small pot. Bring to a boil, then remove from the heat and cool to room temperature.

- Meanwhile, trim the cauliflower into small florets and place in a 4-pint glass jar. Pour the vinegar mixture into the jar, then toss in the nigella seeds and garlic. Ferment in the refrigerator for at least 1 week

---

RED ONION

Makes about 1 quart

8 medium red onions, thinly sliced
1 small red beet, sliced into paper-thin rounds
1 bay leaf
1 small star anise
1 small cinnamon stick
2 cups white vinegar
1 cup sugar

- Place the onions, beet, bay leaf, star anise, and cinnamon stick in a 1-quart glass jar. Whisk together the vinegar and sugar in a small bowl and pour over the red onions.

- Allow to ferment for at least 1 week in the refrigerator.

MY AIOLIS

AIOLI IS BASICALLY A FANCY NAME FOR MAYONNAISE. TECHNICALLY, AIOLI IS AN emulsion of eggs (both whites and yolks), acids, oil, garlic, sugar, and salt. To this base, you can add roasted garlic, saffron, or just about anything else to create the version of aioli you choose. Here are three options, but I encourage you to experiment and make your own.

LEMON AIOLI

Makes about 2 cups

1 large egg
1½ cups canola oil
¼ cup fresh lemon juice
Zest of 2 lemons
¼ teaspoon ground turmeric
1 teaspoon sugar
1½ teaspoons kosher salt

- Place the egg in a food processor and, with the machine running, slowly pour in the canola oil in a thin, steady stream. The mixture will start to thicken into an almost custardlike consistency.

- After you finish adding the oil, turn off the food processor and add the lemon juice, zest, turmeric, sugar, and salt. Run the food processor just long enough to incorporate all the seasonings, about 30 seconds.

- The aioli can be stored in an airtight container in the refrigerator for up to 3 days.

GARLIC AIOLI

Makes about 2 cups

1 clove Roasted Garlic (page 273)
1 garlic clove
Kosher salt
1 large egg
1½ cups canola oil
2 tablespoons fresh lemon juice
2 tablespoons water
1 teaspoon sugar

- Mash up both garlic cloves with a fork until they start to resemble a paste. Sprinkling a teeny bit of salt on the raw garlic clove will help this process along. Set aside.

- Place the egg in a food processor. With the machine running, slowly drizzle in the canola oil. Once the mixture is thick and creamy, add the garlic paste, lemon juice, water, sugar, and 1½ teaspoons salt. Run the food processor just long enough to thoroughly combine the garlic paste with the aioli, about 1 minute.

- The aioli can be stored in an airtight container in the refrigerator for up to 3 days.

SAFFRON AIOLI

Makes about 2 cups

1 cup white wine vinegar

1 small shallot, finely chopped

1 garlic clove, finely chopped

½ teaspoon chile flakes

Pinch of saffron threads

1 large egg

1½ cups canola oil

2 tablespoons fresh lemon juice

2 tablespoons water

1½ teaspoons sugar

2 teaspoons kosher salt

1 teaspoon ground turmeric

- Combine the vinegar, shallot, garlic, chile flakes, and saffron in a small saucepan. Bring to a boil, then lower the heat and simmer until the vinegar is reduced almost to nothing, 15 to 20 minutes. Remove from the heat, transfer the mixture to a food processor, and puree until it reaches a pastelike consistency. Scrape into a bowl using a rubber spatula and set it aside.

- Add the egg to the same food processor, and, with the machine running, gradually add the oil in a very thin, steady stream. After you finish adding the oil, turn off the processor and add the saffron paste, lemon juice, water, sugar, salt, and turmeric. Run the processor just long enough to blend in the saffron paste, about 1 minute.

- The aioli can be stored in an airtight container in the refrigerator for up to 3 days.

LABNE

Makes about 3 cups

LABNE IS HARD TO DESCRIBE, but it's essentially Arabic soft cheese that is made out of yogurt. Typically it's made with goat's milk, but here I use cow's. And to make it even easier, I suggest starting with simple yogurt that you then drain through cheesecloth overnight. If you want your labne harder, in round balls, allow it to drain even longer, so it toughens and becomes malleable. In other words, the longer you drain it, the harder it gets—anywhere from a soft cream-cheese-like spread to a solid nugget.

4 cups plain yogurt
1 tablespoon kosher salt
Olive oil
Za'atar seasoning (see Note, page 77)

- Mix together the yogurt and salt in a large bowl. Line a large-mesh sieve with 3 layers of cheesecloth and rest the sieve over a medium bowl. Scrape the yogurt onto the cheesecloth and allow the mixture to drain overnight in the refrigerator.

- Store the labne in an airtight container in the refrigerator for up to 1 week. Garnish with olive oil and za'atar before serving.

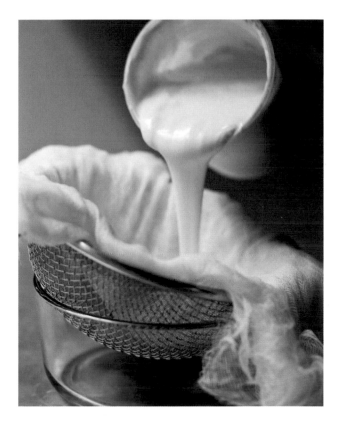

MEXITERRANEAN ADOBO

Makes about 5 cups

THIS MIXTURE OF DRY SPICES is filled with garlic, paprika, cumin, and three kinds of chile. It's terrific on steak, but also on vegetables—especially when cooking out on the grill. It's also wonderful on chicken breast. I wouldn't think of eating meat without it.

2 cups granulated sugar
1 cup raw (turbinado) sugar
1/2 cup ancho chile powder
1/2 cup New Mexican chile powder
1/2 cup sweet Hungarian paprika
1/4 cup chipotle powder
1/3 cup onion powder
1/3 cup garlic powder
3/4 tablespoons hickory seasoning
2 tablespoons ground cumin

- Combine all the ingredients in a large bowl and mix thoroughly. Store in an airtight container at room temperature for up to a few months—I bet it won't last that long.

WORLD'S BEST HARISSA

Makes about 2½ cups

THINK OF HARISSA AS A modern-day gourmet hot sauce—or, if you prefer, as an update to Tabasco: it can be used on anything, in anything, and with anything, and will always make it better. My harissa can be used as a sauce, a paste, or a broth for slow cooking. The main ingredients are garlic and an array of spices, most notably red pepper (cayenne).

10 garlic cloves
1 large roasted red bell pepper, peeled, cored, and seeded
1 1/4 cups canola oil
1/4 cup tomato paste
1/2 cup ground cumin
1/3 cup cayenne
1/3 cup sweet Hungarian paprika
1/4 cup ground caraway
2 tablespoons kosher salt

- Combine the garlic, bell pepper, 1 cup of the oil, and the tomato paste in a food processor. Pulse until the mixture is almost pureed.

- Add the cumin, cayenne, paprika, caraway, and salt. Slowly drizzle in the remaining 1/4 cup oil while the machine is running. Keep processing until the harissa is completely pureed and all the ingredients are thoroughly combined.

- Store the harissa in an airtight container in the refrigerator for up to 3 months.

ROASTED GARLIC

THE TRADITIONAL WAY TO roast garlic is in the oven. But here's an easier version: peel the bulb ahead of time instead of after and then braise it in oil. I didn't forget to put any quantities in this recipe. Roast as many garlic cloves as you'd like.

Garlic cloves
Canola oil

- Peel each garlic clove and place it in a saucepan. Pour in just enough canola oil to cover the cloves completely.

- Place the pan over a very low—and I mean *low*—flame. Simmer until the garlic cloves are tender and brown spots start to appear, 25 to 30 minutes. Remove from the heat and cool completely before transferring the garlic to an airtight container with just enough oil to cover the cloves.

- I store the roasted garlic in a jar in the refrigerator for up to 2 weeks. And I *never* throw away the rest of the oil, because it's great for brushing on slices of ciabatta right before grilling them. Just make sure to store the oil in the refrigerator as well, and this will keep much longer than a few weeks.

POMEGRANATE CONFITURE

Makes about 2 cups

FOR THIS RECIPE YOU'LL NEED to learn how to seed a pomegranate. It's easier than you think. Slice the pomegranate in half and then hold it upside down (i.e., skin side up) in your hand. Then do your best Ringo Starr imitation and bang the living daylights out of it with a spoon, and watch as the seeds rain down into your mixing bowl.

6 cups pomegranate seeds (from about 10 pomegranates)
6 cups sugar
¼ cup water

- Place the seeds, sugar, and water in a medium saucepan and bring the mixture to a boil. Lower the heat to simmer and cook until thick, like syrup, about 35 minutes. Stir the mixture occasionally to prevent the bottom from burning. Remove from the heat and cool completely.

- Store in an airtight container in the refrigerator for up to 1 year. Not only is the confiture great on slices of toast and sandwiches, it does wonders with so many delicious chicken dishes, like Mom's Chicken with Pomegranate and Walnuts (page 213).

S'CHUG

(DAD'S HOT, HOT, HOT SAUCE)

Makes about 1½ cups

AS I MENTIONED EARLIER, **MY** father actually takes this homemade sauce with him to restaurants. In the old days, he'd make his hot sauce, called *s'chug*, in a meat grinder, but a food processor works just as well. Aside from the heart-pounding, eye-watering taste, this dish is very special to me because it's the only recipe that belongs completely to my dad, without so much as a word from my mother. Even today, my father cleans the cilantro, picks his own chile in the spice market, peels the garlic, and grinds it all by himself—a true labor of love! I can't eat *s'chug* without thinking about him.

10 garlic cloves, coarsely chopped
4 dried red chiles
Seeds from 2 cardamom pods
3 jalapeño chiles, cored, seeded, and coarsely chopped
2 cups packed fresh cilantro leaves
1 teaspoon kosher salt
¼ teaspoon ground cumin
¾ cup canola oil

- Combine all the ingredients in a food processor and pulse until finely chopped. Then run the machine continuously until the sauce is smooth.

- Transfer the hot sauce to an airtight container and store in the refrigerator for up to 1 month.

PERFECT PRESERVED LEMONS

SURE, THEY TAKE NINETY DAYS to make. But they're such an amazing addition to so many different kinds of dishes that it's totally worth the wait. And actual prep time is only 20 minutes. Preserved Lemons are essential to the Casablanca Catch (page 23) and Seared Snapper with Red Pepper Lemon Sauce and Rice Cakes (page 251), but they're equally fantastic with chicken—really, with anything.

3 cups kosher salt

1 cup sugar

½ tablespoon coriander seeds

1½ teaspoons black peppercorns

¼ teaspoon ground turmeric

¼ teaspoon sweet Hungarian paprika

12 to 16 lemons, or more

2 bay leaves

- Mix together the salt, sugar, coriander seeds, peppercorns, turmeric, and paprika in a large bowl. Place half of the mixture at the bottom of a 1-gallon glass jar with a tight-fitting lid.

- Cut the lemons into wedges and place them inside the jar, squeezing the juices into the jar as you throw them in. It's important to pack the lemons in the jar with little room around them, so there is no air to oxidize them. Don't worry about squishing the lemons; they like it this way. Next add the bay leaves, the remaining salt mixture, and top it off with just enough water to fill it to the rim. Seal the jar and forget about it for the next 3 months or so. Well, remember it once in a while and gently flip the jar upside down a few times to make sure all the flavors are mixing together. The lemons are ready when the skin is soft.

- Before you open the jar, the preserved lemons can be stored at room temperature, but once they are ready, it's best to store them in the refrigerator, where they will keep for at least 6 months. Be sure to rinse away the excess salt from the lemons prior to each use and discard the pulp.

SIMPLE SYRUP

Makes about 4 cups

4 cups water
4 cups sugar

- Combine the water and sugar in a large pot and simmer until the sugar is completely dissolved, about 7 minutes. Remove from the heat and cool to room temperature.

- The syrup can be stored in an airtight container in the refrigerator for up to 1 week.

MINT SYRUP

Makes about 4 cups

YOU CAN BUY SIMPLE SYRUP at most markets, but it's even easier to make. The mint adds a refreshing twist that's perfect in tea and cocktails.

4 cups water
4 cups sugar
1 large bunch fresh mint

- Combine the water and sugar in a large pot and simmer until the sugar is completely dissolved, about 7 minutes. Remove from the heat and stir in the mint, stems and all. Set aside to allow the flavors to infuse for a few hours, then discard the mint and store the syrup in an airtight container in the refrigerator for up to 1 week.

ROSE SYRUP

Makes about 1½ cups

THIS AROMATIC SYRUP GOES with so many Middle Eastern dishes. In this book I call for it in the baklava and *kanafeh* recipes (pages 224 and 256, respectively), but try incorporating it into beverages too. I love just a few drops in lemonade or Rosetta, a popular almond drink in Israel.

1 cup water
2 cups sugar
¼ cup honey
One 3-inch strip orange zest
1 cardamom pod
¼ teaspoon rose water

- Combine the water, sugar, honey, orange zest, and cardamom in a medium saucepan. Simmer over low heat until the sugar is completely dissolved. Remove from the heat, stir in the rose water, and discard the orange zest and cardamom pod.

- Transfer the syrup to an airtight container and chill in the refrigerator for up 24 hours.

THANK YOU

This book could not have happened without the love and support of family, friends, and the staff at Artisan.

My editor, Lia Ronnen, believed in this project from the start. After working with her for two years, I'm convinced we're of one mind. She is my editor but also my friend.

My agent, Susie Finesman, was the first to suggest I write a cookbook. Her ambition and sass were critical to getting this project off the ground.

Joel Chasnoff captured my voice and turned into words the stories that best define me—and with excellent grammar, no less. Dhale Pomes tasted and prepared almost every recipe in this book; I am grateful for her time and taste buds.

Guy Zarfati is my chef at Balaboosta and best friend for twenty years. He encouraged me from our earliest days in culinary school and taught me what true friendship is all about.

For better or for worse, it is because of my parents, Ziona and Menashe, that I can call myself the *balaboosta* I am today. In a similar vein, my brother, Elon, and big sister, Dorit, have provided me with strength, humor, and (in Dorit's case, at least) a few of my favorite recipes.

My children, Liam and Mika, continue to teach me how important it is to remain a child at heart. They may not understand why I need to work as hard as I do. Still, I'm keeping them.

I want to thank Ann Bramson, Michelle Ishay-Cohen, Trent Duffy, Bridget Heiking, Allison McGeehon, and Nancy Murray at Artisan, all of whom worked tirelessly on behalf of the book and kept this project on the rails; Quentin Bacon for the stunning photographs; Paul Kepple and Ralph Geroni for the beautiful design; George Lange for the wonderful promotional video; Lorry Balter and Aaron Matalon, for simply believing; my staff at Balaboosta and Taïm; and the various *balaboostas* in my life who continue to inspire me.

Finally, I wish to thank my husband, Stefan . . . for everything.

INDEX

CONVERSION CHART

Here are rounded-off equivalents between the metric system and the traditional systems used in the United States to measure weight and volume.

WEIGHTS

US/UK	Metric
¼ oz	7 g
½ oz	15 g
1 oz	30 g
2 oz	55 g
3 oz	85 g
4 oz	115 g
5 oz	140 g
6 oz	170 g
7 oz	200 g
8 oz (½ lb)	225 g
9 oz	255 g
10 oz	285 g
11 oz	310 g
12 oz	340 g
13 oz	370 g
14 oz	400 g
15 oz	425 g
16 oz (1 lb)	450 g

VOLUME

American	Imperial	Metric
¼ tsp		1.25 ml
½ tsp		2.5 ml
1 tsp		5 ml
½ Tbsp (1½ tsp)		7.5 ml
1 Tbsp (3 tsp)		15 ml
¼ cup (4 Tbsp)	2 fl oz	60 ml
⅓ cup (5 Tbsp)	2½ fl oz	75 ml
½ cup (8 Tbsp)	4 fl oz	125 ml
⅔ cup (10 Tbsp)	5 fl oz	150 ml
¾ cup (12 Tbsp)	6 fl oz	175 ml
1 cup (16 Tbsp)	8 fl oz	250 ml
1¼ cups	10 fl oz	300 ml
1½ cups	12 fl oz	350 ml
1 pint (2 cups)	16 fl oz	500 ml
2½ cups	20 fl oz (1 pint)	625 ml
5 cups	40 fl oz (1 qt)	1.25 l

OVEN TEMPERATURES

	°F	°C	Gas Mark
VERY COOL	250–275	130–140	½–1
COOL	300	148	2
WARM	325	163	3
MEDIUM	350	177	4
MEDIUM HOT	375–400	190–204	5–6
HOT	425	218	7
VERY HOT	450–475	232–245	8–9